THE
GENUINE
JESUS

Received by James E. Padgett
and Dr. Daniel G. Samuels

Compiled by Alan Ross

Edited by Richard Baker

Historical Contribution
Ronald Henderson

To Harin,
Bless you for
your help and
kindness, Alan
Ross

ISBN # 0-9617038-0-6

First Edition

Includes bibliographical references

Printed in the USA

Alan Ross Publications (East Coast)
1438 W. Lantana Road #401
Lantana, FL 33462
(888) 937- 0411

Alan Ross Publications (West Coast)
P.O. Box 1203
Manhattan Beach, CA 90266
(888) 937- 0411

(United Kingdom)
Alan Ross Publications
88 Camden Road
London NW1 9EA
0171 - 485 0285

e-mail: alanross@aol.com
www.thegenuinejesus.com

Dedication

I dedicate this book to my dearest friends of this spiritual path: to Alese Jones a lovely lady who means so much to me in this work, to Gregory Boster a good friend who gave me my first book of these teachings and to Isaiah Watkins a great spiritual teacher who has been like a father to me.

CONTENTS

THE REAPPEARANCE

THE SECOND COMING

THE TEACHINGS

ACKNOWLEDGEMENTS

I would like to acknowledge Mr. James E. Padgett for his dedication as the chosen instrument of Jesus to bring his revelation to the world and Dr. Leslie R. Stone for his work as first publisher of the writings. Also Dr. Daniel G. Samuels who was the second instrument and a founding trustee of the Dr. Leslie R. Stone Foundation in 1954.

In 1958 the Dr. Leslie R. Stone Foundation's name was changed to the Foundation Church of the New Birth. Its purpose is to preserve, reprint and disseminate the messages from Jesus in their originally transcribed form. The present day trustees continue to carry forward the religious functions and programs set into motion by the founding trustees. Since the first printing in 1940 many thousands of books have been published and disseminated to various parts of the world.

INTRODUCTION

S ince his appearance in Palestine nearly two thousand years ago, the story of the man from Galilee has spread to all corners of the globe. His life has inspired artists and  musicians to new heights. Great houses of worship have been erected to his glory and all in adoration for his having lived a perfect life.

Who then was this man? Was he the result of a virgin birth? Is he God incarnate? Did he come to suffer and die as payment for the sins of humanity? Jesus was not born of a virgin but in the normal way. He is not God, nor did he come to pay a price for sin. Instead he was the first human to attain through prayer an immortal soul filled with the Essence of God, Divine Love. In this way he was the Christ, the first true Son of God and the Messiah.

Jesus did sacrifice himself but in a way that was never relayed or understood by the writers of the New Testament. He gave up the opportunity to have a home and family of his own and to lead the quiet pursuits of a Nazarene carpenter. Instead he endured the hatred and opposition of those who did not understand him. He lived a life of constant travel and often had no place to lay his head.

The doctrine of Jesus' blood sacrifice is just one of many that is pure speculation on the part of the Church philosophers and cannot be satisfactorily explained by the priests and leaders. Their followers are told to accept this doctrine as well as others on faith alone, but for many people faith as an explanation is not enough. Many of these people have sought answers outside the established churches, myself included. In 1982 my search for answers led me to a small group of spiritualists in Santa Cruz, California, where I was living at the time. Their faith was based on a great spiritual event which had taken place at the beginning of the century in the form of extraordinary channeled messages originating from Jesus of Nazareth. In an early message Jesus states, "The work I am now engaged in represents a new and important revelation from the world of spirits." Once again Jesus had come to the earth only this time in spirit form from high up in his heaven to be close to a certain lawyer named James Padgett whom he used to record his thoughts by the means of automatic writing.

James Padgett had been a practical lawyer for thirty-five years prior to his becoming a medium. His mediumship began

in 1914 shortly after the loss of his wife Helen. Padgett loved his wife dearly and her passing left a great void in his life. One evening a friend who knew of his loneliness suggested they attend a spiritualist meeting in the hope of making contact with her. Padgett reluctantly accepted because at the time he had had no prior experience with the supernatural having been raised in the orthodox Methodist Church.

James E. Padgett   Nevertheless, he accompanied his friend to the meeting held at the home of a Mrs. Maltby. There she described Helen perfectly and told Padgett that his wife had the ability to write messages from the spirit world and that she would control him if he would only try. In the evenings that followed Padgett sat patiently at his desk with pencil in hand thinking of Helen and longing to write her words. Many frustrating nights went by with no results until one evening his hand moved and produced what he called fish hooks and hangers. Eventually he scribbled out a short note signed "Helen." In the note Helen encouraged her husband to continue his efforts to receive her thoughts and to believe that it was really she.

Because of his legal background, Padgett was skeptical that these were genuine communications from his departed wife. He asked Helen for proof and she responded by sending information of incidents in their lives which Padgett recognized could only have been known to both of them. Padgett thought possibly the information could be coming from his own mind but the nature of the material was foreign to his religious training.

After reading books on the subject of Spiritualism and attending meetings, Padgett learned that spirits given the opportunity and under the right conditions can communicate with mortals. He was advised through this means to continue taking messages while learning more about the spirit world. Prior to his writing sessions Padgett could feel his wife's presence intensely which produced in him a profound feeling of happiness. In time he became compelled to accept the writings as proof that his wife was alive and well, fully conscious, living in another dimension and that she was able to send her thoughts to him and he was able to write them down.

Helen's letters then took a turn from the personal to the spiritual. She told her husband that his ability to write messages from spirits was known in the highest spheres of the spirit world and that Jesus of Nazareth and his disciples wanted to use his talent to bring spiritual truth and enlightenment to the world. Soon after, Padgett wrote a message from Jesus stating, "My purpose for using you is to correct many of the inaccuracies which have been recorded in the New Testament about my life, my mission and my death."

Jesus explains that he had been trying for centuries to find someone he could use to accurately record the corrections to the New Testament. He had found many mediums in the past who were far more gifted than Padgett, but because they thought it impossible for him to write through them or, due to their religious beliefs and dogmas, they had refused to submit to his prompting. Padgett on the other hand believed in his wife's letters that Jesus would come to him.

Padgett had not been selected for his goodness or freedom from sin compared to other mortals (there were many who were more spiritually evolved than he), but because he possessed a natural psychic gift that could be developed, and that he had the ability to control his mind—to keep it passive and allow the spirits' messages to pass through his brain to manipulate his hand to write the words. Padgett was reassured by Jesus that he would not have to submit his will to the control of any spirit writing through him and that he would always be in full consciousness and control of his faculties while his psychic ability was being used. Therefore, whenever he chose, he would be able to interrupt or discontinue the writing which he did from time to time in order to ask questions.

Padgett was instructed by Jesus to pray often for Divine Love to enter his soul which would increase his psychic power and give his mediumship a very high quality of receptivity. This would enable Jesus to form the necessary rapport with Padgett to accurately transmit his thoughts to him. Prior to the writing sessions Padgett would feel the Divine Love in his soul with great intensity. His devotion to this work enabled him to create the optimum conditions by purifying his mind of material thoughts in order to receive all nature of intellectual, moral and spiritual messages. As his soul continued to purify through the reception of Divine Love, the meaning and content of the messages became ever clearer to him.

It may seem surprising to some spiritualists that Jesus was able to make direct contact with Padgett instead of using the filtering down method whereby the message from a high spirit is passed down from spirit to spirit until it reaches the mortal medium. Jesus deemed this method not reliable enough for the type of knowledge he wished to communicate. He knew that he needed a direct medium in order that his meaning would not be misrepresented as had been the case in the past.

After Jesus completed his great messages to correct the Bible, other spirits were allowed to take advantage of Padgett's talent. In one such message from John, Apostle of Jesus, he describes Jesus' physical appearance at the time of his ministry. John says, "I have never heard of any portrait having been painted of Jesus while he lived on earth. The oldest portraits in existence were not made until years after his death and by men who could not have gotten a description from anyone who had seen him.

As were the rest of us who were his disciples, the Master was a Jew, however, he had in him a condition of soul that to a large extent determined and fashioned his appearance. His eyes were not dark or brown, but a violet blue. His hair was light and inclined to be auburn and he wore it parted in the middle and it reached to his shoulders and was somewhat curly, a beautiful head of hair which seemed to be full of life. His nose was straight but prominent. His beard was the color of his hair, and he never had a razor on his face. His forehead was not so very high or broad but was well shaped and somewhat effeminate. Surprisingly, this was an indication that he did not have as much mental development as one might suppose. But I must tell you that his knowledge was not the knowledge of the brain but of the soul."

Jesus traveled the roads and footpaths of Palestine as the living example of the New Covenant of the Heart which God had promised many centuries before through His prophets. The Divine Love as perceived through the spiritual vision of Hosea, Isaiah, Jeremiah, and Ezekiel had now become a reality of the human heart and was exemplified in all its Divine splendor and beauty in Jesus. Jesus loved all people with a love that showed itself in kindness, in the service of helping others, in healing wounds and sickness, in alleviating sorrow and in giving sympathy and comfort. He brought hope and taught salvation to thousands. He was the light to the Jewish nation, the one who would show the way to God and peace.

The messages from Jesus were sent for the emerging new religion of Spiritualism because it more than any other could accept communications of such an unusual nature. If Jesus' teachings had been revealed to and embraced by Spiritualism they would have completed its philosophy at the time when it was at the pinnacle of its popularity. This would have empowered its mediums and healers to enable Spiritualism to take its rightful place among the world's great religions. The timing was ideal for new revelation, World War I was ragging and Jesus had been expected by many. As a matter of fact as far back as 1876, the Jehovah Witnesses realized that Bible prophecy marked the year 1914, as a time when major events would take place that would have far-reaching effects on human affairs. I believe Jesus did come at the prescribed time but not in the form that he was expected.

It appears that James Padgett confided mainly in his closest friends Dr. Leslie Stone, Mr. Eugene Morgan, and Dr. Goerger. I feel it is fair to assume that if he had made a public statement of his mediumship, some evidence of the publicity would have survived from the heaps that one would expect a lawyer of James Padgett's repute to receive had he claimed that in the evenings after work he would retreat to his study to write the "Second Coming" from Jesus of the Bible. After all, most of the original automatic writings now yellowed with age on legal pads have survived, why not the newspaper clippings. It is because there are none, no publicity, no disbarment hearings, no sanity hearings not a whisper. Padgett may have known about Judge John Edmonds of the New York State Superior Court who some years earlier was forced to resign from the bench for speaking out on the behalf of Spiritualism. There is, however, evidence of a letter Padgett wrote describing his mediumship to a Dr. George H. Gilbert, Ph.D., D.D., who had written an article in Biblical World entitled "Christianizing the Bible" which impressed him. The following is an excerpt from that letter dated December 28, 1915.

"I will frankly say that I refused for a long time to believe that these messages came from Jesus because God, while He had the power as I believed, would not engage in doing such a thing. But the evidence of the truth of the origin of these messages became so convincing not only from the great number and positiveness of the spirit witnesses, but from the inherent and unusual merits of the contents of the messages that I was forced to believe, and I now say to you that I believe in the truth of these communications with as little doubt as I ever believed in the truth of a fact established by the most positive evidence in court". The great object of these messages from Jesus as he wrote is to make a revelation of the truths of his Father. He asserts that the Bible does not contain his real teachings as he disclosed them while on earth, that many things that he said are not therein contained, and many things that are ascribed to him therein he did not say at all. Jesus wants his teachings made known to mankind, and I must say that many of these which he has already written, I have never before heard of, and I have studied the Bible to some extent. One thing in particular impressed me and that is his bringing "life and immortality to light". The Bible does not state it, and I have not been able to find in any commentaries on the Bible an explanation of it."

Dr. Leslie R. Stone

With Padgett's passing in 1923, Dr. Stone became the publisher of his works. Dr. Stone was born in Aldershot, Hampshire, in 1876 and emigrated to Canada in 1903 where he was introduced to Spiritualism. In the fall of 1914 he relocated to Washington, D.C. where he became acquainted with Mr. James Padgett. Dr. Stone was often present during his writing sessions and observed that the spirits' thoughts

Sample of James Padgett's automatic writing

came in such a rapid sweep of connected words Padgett had no time for thought. In fact Padgett insisted that he had no clear idea of what his pencil was writing until he read the messages afterwards.

It was a considerable undertaking for Dr. Stone to publish the first book of writings because with Padgett's automatic writing the words were interconnected without breaks or punctuation, nevertheless, he persevered and completed his book in 1940. By then American Spiritualism was a mere shadow of its former self, its glory days were gone due for the most part to the successful campaign by the celebrated escape artist Harry Houdini to expose fraudulent mediums. Houdini succeeded to turn public opinion against the spiritualist mediums which contributed sharply to Spiritualism's decline. Spiritualism is little known today, although it influenced the New Thought Movement which was the early forerunner of today's New Age Movement.

James Padgett is gone, but his writings have survive; however, they are not widely known. Jesus wants these teachings made available to all people it is for this reason I have published *The Genuine Jesus* to serve as an introduction to James Padgett's vast legacy of scientific, philosophical and religious writings as they are contained in four printed volumes.

I present *The Genuine Jesus* to you in the first person just as Mr. Padgett and later his successor, Dr. Daniel G. Samuels, received the writings from Jesus. All of the material in this autobiography originated from Jesus except for a small portion which came from other spirit authors who were present at the time this story took place. Because the more than one hundred original notes, letters and sermons were not delivered in any particular order, I arranged them to follow the Gospels of the New Testament and wrote connecting sentences to maintain the continuity of the story. All of the Bible references were verified using the King James version of the Bible.

I hope you will find *The Genuine Jesus* thought-provoking and of value to you on your spiritual journey.

Alan Ross

BIRTH AND YOUTH

Annunciation

I am here to let you know that I am that Jesus of Nazareth who walked the roads of Palestine with my disciples in the days of Herod Antipas and the Roman centurions and soldiers who filled Jerusalem. My name in Hebrew is Jeshua ben Joseph for I was named after Joshua ben Nun, a man who led his people to the promised land of Canaan. My mother's name was Miriam for the Hebrews did not have the name Mary in their dialect, and due to the translation Miriam became Mary.

My mother told me that the story of the angel of God coming to her and telling her that she must submit to the birth of a child by the Holy Spirit and that as a virgin she would give birth to that child is not true (Luke 1:31).

The early Christian editors were seeking for something in the Old Testament writings to support their theories of a virgin birth for the "Christ" to convert their pagan compatriots. The passage adopted, "Behold, the young woman is with child and will bear a son and will call his name Immanuel" (Isaiah 7:14-16). This sentence was taken out of context and the Hebrew word alma (a young woman) was given the meaning "virgin" by the Greek and Latin translators so that the thought expressed was that of a virgin birth, so popular in ancient religions. This prophecy of Isaiah did not refer to me but to a child born during his time.

The concept of the virgin birth was borrowed from legend, here I may cite the birth of Horus among the Egyptians. The Greeks also conceived of gods being born in supernatural ways and without the benefit of mortal fathers. It was through the reading of these Greek legends that the idea of making my mother a virgin was secured. Greek legends told of a number of goddesses who gave birth to sons although they themselves were virgins. I can name such an instance of Danae who gave birth to Perseus without the benefit of a human mate, but instead she was supposedly impregnated by Zeus who came to her in a shower of gold from the sky.

This concept actually goes back to the Buddhist religion. In their writings which deal with the conception of the Buddha, it is described how Buddha's mother was transported to a mythical heaven and there impregnated in a mystical way with the child, Buddha, without the aid of a husband. The writer of the Gospel was very much affected by this story (Luke 1:35) and in his wish to give me supernatural status, ascribed events to me analogous with what he found in the writings on the Buddha.

Joseph

My father, Joseph, was not a peasant or man of the people, but was a man of considerable spiritual training inasmuch as he held a fine social position as a descendant of some of the great kings of Israel, notably David and Solomon. He was a devout Jew, a Pharisee at heart, who sought to uphold the Jewish traditions based upon strict observance of Hebrew law. He never supposed at any time that I was not his child, for he was a young man and not the decrepit, impotent old man that he has been made out to be. He was legally married to my mother and, as a matter of fact, their wedding had all the color, pageantry and love that went with that ancient Hebrew rite.

The story of the angel's coming to Joseph and telling him that he must not put my mother away because of appearances (Matthew 1:19) is not true. Never in any of my conversations with him did he intimate that such a thing had happened. Furthermore, in later years a century or so after my death the idea became popular with the

Christian leaders to make the world believe that my mother never had any other children. They stated instead that my brothers James and Jude were my cousins. They invented the story in which my mother, Mary, had a sister with the same name who married the brother of my father and this supposed brother was called Alphaeus. In this way these later writers hoped to induce Christians to believe that my mother had lived as a virgin all her life.

Star of Bethlehem

The Bible's account of my birth in Bethlehem is substantially accurate and was the fulfillment of Micah's  prophesy (Micah 5:2). My mother gave birth to me in a stable on the outskirts of the village, not because my parents were too poor to afford better lodgings for my father had a certain amount of money accruing to him through his trade, but because it was census time and Bethlehem was small with only one inn and there were no rooms available (Luke 2:7).

Two years before my birth a bright star was seen in the eastern skies which caused a great deal of excitement and anxiety in the land. The Star of Bethlehem, as it is known, in reality was an exploding star, or supernova, which caused considerable light in the sky. The three wise men who saw the star, were astrologers with a knowledge of ancient Chaldean astrological lore and of the Hebrew writings determined that a great event was to take place as a result of the appearance of the bright light in the heavens. It had been predicted that a "King of the Jews" was to be born in Judea (Matthew 2:2). This seemed to them all the more true since the light pointed in a westerly direction.

The wise men set out for Jerusalem, the capital of Judea, but it was some time before they reached their destination. This was due to the preparations and the actual journey to cross the Arabian Desert. The light from the star was no longer with them having burned out about two weeks after it had appeared. The three wise men purchased gifts of frankincense and myrrh in addition to a small amount of gold while on their way across the desert (Matthew 2:11).

I was born exactly as other babies are born shortly after midnight on January 7th by the western calendar. In keeping with tradition my father celebrated the birth of his first-born by going out into the streets and nearby countryside to look for others who might help him to welcome his newborn son. He invited some shepherds (Luke 2:15) for wine and cake and they joined with my father in offering songs of praise and thanksgiving to God for my safe delivery and for my mother's well-being. Soon after I was presented at the Temple in Jerusalem as was the custom for a newborn of the Chassidic sect (Luke 2:22).

When the wise men reached Jerusalem, they went first to the Temple and inquired about the birth of the one who  would be "King of the Jews". The high priests sent them to King Herod, for the priests feared any mention of a Jewish king was political in nature and might be offensive to Herod with whom they were allied for the maintenance of the status quo in Jerusalem. After they saw Herod, the wise men made their way to Bethlehem to pay their respects to me and make their offering. They found my birth to be a humble one as they had expected (Luke 2:12). They did not show themselves in Bethlehem until six weeks after my birth, my mother had just completed her term of purification which lasted forty days.

Instead of returning to Herod, the Magi departed for the East at the same time my family fled to Egypt. When Herod learned that they had disappeared, he took alarm

and issued a decree to slaughter all of the infants in the
town and vicinity. He made inquiries to learn the date of
the so-called "Star of Bethlehem" and discovered that it
had first appeared two years before. This determined the
ages of the Hebrew children which he would have put to
the sword for the purpose to eliminate any possibility of
the appearance of the Jewish Deliverer of the prophecies
(Matthew 2:16).

Flight to Egypt

Herod's soldiers did not catch my family because my
father had been quick to understand the temper of Herod

and his possible edict against me.
He hastened to depart to Egypt
with me and my mother using the
funds my father had prior to him
reaching Bethlehem. My mother
was able to make the journey for
she had recovered from her lying-
in period. Had Herod's edict come earlier, my father
would not have been able to flee to Egypt because it
would have been too soon after my mother's delivery for
her to travel.

Upon our arrival in Egypt my father sought the home
of a Jewish relative who lived in Heliopolis, a town not far
from Cairo. He welcomed us and enabled our family to
make our start in this new land. There was quite a
community of Jewish people there, and we congregated
together for safety as well as for social life. There was a
place for worship, a place for the cleansing of women and
also an elementary school for the teaching of reading and
writing to enable youngsters to learn the Scriptures.

My father pursued his occupation as a carpenter to
support us. After a while he was able to set up and
establish his trade quite successfully and made his
household a comfortable one with all the conveniences
available to workmen of the day. When I was old enough,

I attended the common school where I learned those things which had to do with the religion of the Jews. While in Egypt my parents had four other sons and three daughters.

Return to Palestine

As the years passed, my mother became homesick for her people and wanted to return to her home in Palestine. My father was hesitant to dismantle the house in which we had lived for the past ten years and return to the hazards of travel. He was concerned about safety, not only for me, but for the entire family because conditions in Judea continued to be unsettled and unfavorable even after the death of Herod. The ruler, Archelaus, who 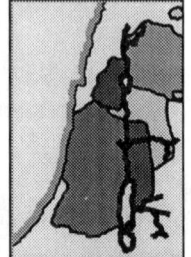 followed Herod, continued his same brutal ways and much blood flowed. There was great unrest and Archelaus, who had been demoted to Ethnarch of Judea, was deposed and sent off in exile to Gaul. Still, conditions did not improve because of the hostility of the people to their Roman overlords.

After much hesitation my father and mother decided to break up their home in Egypt and return to Palestine, and more specifically to Nazareth. No angel came to direct my father to make this return (Matthew 2:19).

Growing Up in Nazareth

While I was growing up in Nazareth, I was a kind and gentle child who loved my mother and father and my brothers and sisters. I was much like other boys with similar feelings and the usual activities of play. The difference was that I was not a sinful boy and did not engage in harmful pranks or sinful deeds because my soul was constituted to know the Love of my Heavenly Father.

In school I was taught those things that had to do with

the religion of the Jews, and some things that were not religious in their nature. I was never taught the philosophy of the Egyptians nor any of the other pagan philosophies, and when it is stated that I received my religious ideas or moral teachings from any of these philosophies, they are mistaken. My early life is shrouded in ignorance and mystery and it needs considerable explanation. My education in matters of religion was derived from the teachings of the Old Testament writings, or rather from Jewish teachers whose used these texts, and also from the Talmud some of which was available in my time.

My father was very eager for me to fulfill the old prophecies and become King of the Jewish Nation. He provided me with all the funds necessary to learn the Scriptures which I did with great thoroughness because of my desire to know the things God had done for my people. My lessons dealt mainly with the prophets. I was a pious student at the synagogue in Nazareth who held dear the words of my teachers. I studied the Jewish Scriptures while I gained increasing spiritual insight and knowledge directly from my Heavenly Father.

I learned in school of a Messiah who would bring redemption to my people. This thought clung to me for God's own Love was already dwelling in my soul because throughout my childhood and boyhood I had had constant yearnings for at-onement with God. I believed in the writings of Jeremiah and the prophets which foretold of the Messiah and of their prophecies of the "New Heart" whereby God would implant His spirit into man's heart and remove the stony heart and replace it with a heart of flesh (Ezekiel 11:19).

I was not in the presence of the Jewish priests being asked questions, nor was I expounding the law to them at the age of twelve (Luke 2:42) for I was not aware of my mission that was yet to come. I never traveled to India or Greece nor any other country. The confusion that has arisen over this alleged story is due to the fact that throughout the years there have been many Hebrews called Jeshua (Jesus). I can name Jeshua, son of Sinch, in connection with the writings which have been published in the non-canonical books of the Bible. I may also mention that there was a Jeshua who, sometime before my appearance in Palestine, incurred the displeasure of the Hebrew authorities and was stoned to death. So you see, in addition to myself, there have been many a mortal called Jeshua and indeed this is a common Hebrew name, and many Hebrews throughout the ages before my time have borne it. Therefore, it is quite possible, and indeed likely, that a man called Jeshua went to the East, studied there and enjoyed friends of various philosophies and beliefs. But I must tell you that I never traveled or studied outside of Palestine for I lived at home all the years of my life working hard helping my father with his trade of carpentry so our family could prosper until I started on my public ministry.

By the time I was twenty, I began to wonder whether I might be this promised Messiah who was prophesied in the Scriptures to show my people the way to their deliverance from sin. The true reality of this came to me later after frequent communions with God through my spiritual senses. I knew in time from the Divine Love growing in my soul that the prophecy of the "New Heart" was being fulfilled in me. I did not have this Divine Love in my soul before my birth but my soul was predisposed to receive It at birth without conscious thought.

As time went on, I understood more and more that I needed to become a prophet to the people and not a great military leader such as my ancestor, King David. This was an understanding of my mission which my father was unable to perceive. He thought of me as a prophet as was John the Baptist; one who would appeal to the people to repent for their sins and to be purified of them, and also one who would turn his attention to the sins of the rulers and remind them of Jehovah.

I saw that many of the Messianic passages in the books

of the prophets could refer to me for I fulfilled many of the requirements such as being from the house of David, being born in Bethlehem and that I came at a time when Judah was a dependency of a foreign power. The prophecies of Daniel also brought the time of the coming of the Messiah to my own days (Daniel 9:25).

When I became convinced of my chosen mission, I tried to tell my family. I would talk to them about my personal relationship with God and of having God's qualities in my own being. They thought that I was deranged for, according to the religious training and knowledge of my people, such a thing was an utter impossibility.

My father was somewhat of a liberal, but he continued to cling to the ideas and beliefs of Hebrew legalisms, customs and ceremonies so dear to the hearts of the Pharisees. Because of his Jewish training, he was not able to understand my true mission which was to bring the message that the Divine Love of the Heavenly Father was the means of bestowing immortality upon His children. My father's religious and national outlook caused a divergence between us as I persisted in my belief and later in my conviction that I had received God's great gift of Divine Love into my soul, and that it was my most high and holy mission to bring the "Glad Tidings" of its bestowal to all humanity.

My sisters, Leah and Rachael, wanted nothing to do with my idealism, they were firm in the old tradition of law and Torah. They thought that possibly I could be a zealot leader going to fight Rome, yet they were a little bewildered because I did not speak belligerently of our enemies, but rather spoke of peace through God's Love in man's soul.

THE MINISTRY

John the Baptist

I had known my cousin, John, quite well since my family's return from Egypt. John was born in June, six months before me, in the neighborhood of Ain Karim which is a small town not far from Jerusalem. The story of the angel's coming to announce the birth of John the Baptist (Luke 1:13) was taken from the story in Genesis of an angel coming to Sarah and telling her that she was to have a son in her old age (Genesis 18:10).

John was the son of Zacharias, a priest who served at the Temple in Jerusalem. John's family was pious and devout, filled with a strict interpretation of the law which the Jews believed had been received from God through Moses. To John's father the laws of Moses and the Ten Commandments represented the most important part of the Jewish religion, and he taught John a strict moral code that he absorbed in his youth which later became the cardinal principles of his brief ministry.

When John was a youth and a young man he worked in the wheat fields to earn a livelihood. His true vocation, however, was that of a prophet in the same sense that Elijah was—that is to say—to proclaim to the rulers and the people to repent their evil ways and to return to the path of righteousness that God had directed the Jews to follow as the great goal of their religion which called for love of God and of one's fellowman.

John was an ascetic who shunned all meat and strong drink. He taught repentance, renunciation of sin, righteousness and love of fellow man. John was a great psychic and had visions of who I was and what my

10

mission was to be.   Later on, as adults, we discussed the way I should be revealed to our people. It was decided that John would be the forerunner and prepare the way for my coming (Matthew 11:10). This meant that he would preach in various places ahead of me so that when I arrived, the people's curiosity would be aroused to know who I was. John began his ministry a few months before mine, and he preached along the banks of the Jordan to those Judeans who would gather to hear him speak. We never preached together in the same place for that would have defeated the purpose of his mission to straighten the path for my subsequent coming (Matthew 3:3).

He never tried to lead a reform movement independent of me, nor was he influenced by the Essenes whose views of purity lead them to live away from the contaminations of civilization in isolated communities where they carried out their religious practices. For, like John, I believed not in retreat from the world but to carry the message of God out to the people. He realized the differences in our missions and spoke of his not being worthy to unloosen my shoes.

My ministry was worked out between us and was part of a prearranged plan. Thus, the Gospel is not true which declares that John did not know me but would anoint the one on whom a dove would descend (John 2:32-33). John anointed me not because of any dove or a voice from heaven, but because he was convinced in his heart that I was the promised Messiah of the Old Testament writings.

I was baptized by stepping into the River Jordan waist deep and, with the waters cupped in his hands, John poured the water upon my head in the symbolic act of coronation as the old Hebrew priests anointed the kings of Israel and Judah. I became the Christ at that moment because I was also anointed by my Heavenly Father with His Divine Love, filling my soul with His Essence and Substance. A voice from the realm of spirit was heard saying, "This is my beloved son in whom I am well pleased" (Matthew 3:17).

The Christian concept of baptism by water eventually superseded the ancient Hebrew custom of sacrifice and became the rite of dedication. Thus, just as I had been baptized in water by John, baptism eventually became the religious symbol of regeneration for Christian salvation. This act predisposed or made the child eligible to receive the redemption of the Holy Spirit, so called by the churches. The baptism of infants has no virtue to save them from their sins or to make them at-one with the Father. The mere fact that water is sprinkled on an infant's head and some blessing pronounced by a preacher does not in any way bring that infant into unison with God. Baptism is of man's creation and means nothing more to God than an outward ceremony that affects the infant merely in regard to his connection with the established earthly church and does not have any effect upon the soul of the infant. The tendency of these ceremonies is to make people neglectful of the great truth; that it is their own efforts that will bring them into harmony with God's laws of love and redemption.

John was a true prophet for he not only preached repentance to all who would listen, but he also thundered against what he considered the evil conduct of Herod for transgressions against God's law of matrimony. John looked upon Herod's marriage to Herodias as illegal (Mark 6:18), an act which could bring down upon his subjects the wrath of God. The Pharisees, to which John belonged, believed their marriage was not legal because no woman, as it was understood, could contract marriage with the brother of a deceased husband when children had been born of the first marriage. Hence Salome, the offspring of Herodias and Herod's step brother, invalidated this marriage to Herod, it was this violation of our levirate marriage law that prompted John's preaching against him.

It is true, of course, that Herodias was incensed against John for, as a member of the ruling class, she was a Sadducee at heart and did not believe in the correctness of his views. She therefore was elated to see him imprisoned and silenced. Herod did not concern himself too much about this part of John's preachings for, while he disagreed with the interpretation of the marriage law, wrangling between Pharisees and Sadducees had been going on for some two centuries and such legalistic disputes did not have the urgency for Herod as this particular one had for Herodias. He was concerned rather with the attitude which the Roman overlords took towards religious meetings which could be a pretext for seditious and rebellious gatherings, and he thought it wise to arrest John the possible cause of disorder in his territory.

Although John was not preaching in territory subject to Herod's jurisdiction, he sent some soldiers in the garb of travelers to seek out John without arousing suspicion. John was sequestered into Herod's land and brought to the fortress of Macherus near the Dead Sea. John was confined there for about ten months, or until Herod's birthday. Herod was not too anxious for John's death, but Herodias wanted it and her request was granted. Solome did dance at this festival (Mark 6:22), but it is not true that her dancing made Herod grant her request for John's death. She never asked for John's decapitation, and I can state that his head was never brought in before the king on a platter. These are fanciful details which students of the Old Testament writings associated with the story of the festival of Purim in which King Ahasuerus vowed to grant Esther anything she asked for at his banquet (Esther 5:6).

The Christ

The Jews expected a Messiah who would lead the people to victory over the Romans in warfare and free their country from foreign rule, but there was no unanimity about who and what the Messiah would be. There were those who thought that coming from God and being sent by Jehovah, he would be a being who would live forever in the flesh. Such was their ignorance of the Jews of things spiritual and their utter carnality of mind that all their religious and spiritual speculations and aspirations were centered entirely upon the material plane. They could not understand that the "Christ" meant the "Christ Principle", or the very Essence of God, which is the Divine Love.

I became the "Christ" at the time of my baptism when the Holy Spirit descended upon me with a great inflowing of Divine Love which entered my soul and transformed it from the image of God, as it was created, into the actual Substance and Essence of God that it had now become. My human soul was now a Divine soul with all the attributes of God's Divine Nature. This is the true meaning of the word "Christ", as it is generally used, referring to the Anointed One or the Messiah or the Saviour.

The "Christ" actually means the principle of God's Divine Love which was made available to humanity as it first appeared in my soul when I proclaimed my mission on earth. It is this Love which saves when it enters the soul of the mortal or spirit. No blood on the cross or any mysterious sacrament of bread and wine will achieve at-onement with God. Only Divine Love has the power to cause the errors and evils of the human soul to be dispelled and thus give a "New Heart" free of sin. Then having the "Christ" in you means having the Divine Love dwelling in your soul. If you read the Epistle of John, the Apostle, you will understand the truth of the saying that the "kingdom of God is within you". For I said, "Herein is love, not that we loved God, but that He loved us" (1 John 4:10). If we love one another with the Divine Love, God dwelleth in us. "God is Love and he that dwelleth in this Love dwelleth in God and God in him" (1 John 4:16). John made it clear that when he spoke of love, he meant Divine Love for all of humanity and where God's Love is, there is God and there will also be God's kingdom.

When I said, "Where two or three are gathered

together in my name, there I will be also" (Matthew 18:20), I did not mean that I would be there in person for this would be impossible. As an individualized spirit, I am limited in my place of occupancy and cannot be in several places at once but the "Christ" can. What I meant by this statement was that where two or three are gathered together for the purpose of seeking Divine Love I would be able to help them feel its influence. I would not need to be present for that purpose for I would be represented by the Holy Spirit. This means that, as the "Christ", I would be with all souls whenever they may seek my help to receive the "Christ Principle" through God's Divine Love.

Now the expression, "Son of Man", applies to me in various places in the New Testament and has a special meaning connected with my messiahship. The term conceived by Ezekiel meant not merely man as a living being but man the created creature of God and therefore "Son of Man", God's created being with whom God could communicate concerning His affairs. Hence, "Son of Man" meant a prophet who could communicate with God and be His spokesman (Ezekiel 2:7). When I came to deliver my message proclaiming the availability of God's Divine Love to humanity, I considered myself to be the "Son of Man" as the prophet of God at the time. In fact, God's Love was in my soul to a considerable degree and I knew what God wanted, therefore I strove to carry out His wishes (John 8:29).

I never said that I was God nor did I ever create any part of the universe. I am merely a spirit of God sent by God to lead men to salvation and show them the way to the heavenly home that He has in keeping for those who receive His Divine Love and the New Heart.

Wilderness and Temptation

I never entered the desert between Jerusalem and the Dead Sea as has been written. Nor did I fast because I did not believe in fasting as a cure against sin. The only fasting I believed in was the fasting of the soul's desire to act in a way contrary to the laws of God. I was not tempted by the devil because there is no devil or Satan (Matthew 4:1). It was the early writers who conceived the figure of a disobedient archangel who warred against God and was thrown out of heaven and became the Prince of Darkness, master of the earth. To this archangel they gave the name "Satan" and endowed him with the ability to change his form and he was cursed by God to become a serpent. Thus, the myth was born that the serpent was symbolic of the Prince of Darkness, or Satan (Revelation 12:9).

There is no such thing as fallen angels who, through ambition or any other reason, revolted against the power of God's government and thereby lost their estate as angels. Never was there any "Lucifer" and never were there any angels thrown from the battlements of heaven into hell. This temptation story was inspired from the Buddha stories. It was taken from the account of the Buddha withstanding the temptations of the powers of the "Prince of Evil" whose attacks against the person of the Buddha were frustrated by His Holiness.

I never said as indicated in the distorted writings of the Gospel of John that the Jews were born of the "devil" and were descendants of a murderer or murderess and had cut themselves off from God (John 8:44). Nor did I call the Jews children of Satan. There were some things I did not come to preach and hatred against man or nation was one of them. This passage has caused a great deal of hatred to be directed against the Jews for their obstinacy in not accepting me as the Messiah.

Proclaimed Messiahship

The one sign that I waited for was the desecration of the Temple prophesied in the Book of Daniel (Daniel 8:14).

When Pontius Pilate began his rule early in the year 26 A.D., he committed as one of his first acts, the deed of desecration of the Temple by ordering his soldiers to enter therein with their idolatrous standards and banners. I knew then that I must come forth and proclaim that I had been anointed the Messiah of God.

I began my public ministry at the age of thirty-three. I did not come to bring something new and revolutionary, but rather I came as the fulfillment of the Scriptures (Luke 4:21). I never entertained the idea of establishing a new religion; for the religion of God had already been established within Judaism. As a religious Jew, I was intent upon living up to the highest ideals of Judaism in the way of that ethical standard of life as preached by our prophets and lawgivers. I was  wholeheartedly attached to my own religious institution, the Temple at Jerusalem, and the assemblies and synagogues of Judaism. I planned to work strictly with the established Hebrew Church to effect needed reforms from within as well as to introduce the "Christ Principle" of the New Heart.

When the time was right, I proclaimed my messiahship to the entire congregation at the synagogue in Nazareth (Luke 4:16). Of course this created a sensation, when I read "The Spirit of Jehovah is upon me and has anointed me to proclaim the "Glad Tidings" (Luke 4:18)," what I meant was that God had appointed me to preach the bestowal of His Divine Love which had been made a reality in my own soul. I also declared to the listeners in the synagogue, "Today is this Scripture fulfilled in your ears" (Luke 4:21). But, the main body of my sermon was based on the sixty-first chapter of Isaiah. When I recited the passage on the delivery of the captives (Isaiah 61:1), I meant freedom from sin, not through adherence to the Mosaic law alone which was the case before my coming, but through the efficacy of the Divine Love of God which reacts upon and transforms the human soul so that it loses its desire for sinful thoughts and deeds.

It is true that I was unable to perform any miracles at that time because of the peculiar situation I was in having lived for twenty-three years in Nazareth. The people who had known me for so long were now suddenly asked to believe that I was the promised Messiah of the Scriptures. This was very difficult for them since I had never healed in my town before, and the people were skeptical that I could suddenly perform what I had not done in the past. There was a strong current of incredulity that prevented me from exercising my healing powers, for faith on the part of the recipient is required to perform the miracle of healing.

Having been anointed the "Christ" through the Divine Love principle, I began to preach this to all who would listen and to teach the way to at-onement with God, and that sin and sickness could now be eliminated through this great gift. My mother loved me very much but was fearful of my mission in that I might bring down upon me the opposition of the Pharisees as well as the Roman legions. On occasion she went with me to see that no harm would come to me. One time she came with some of my brothers and sisters to urge me to give up my mission and come back to Nazareth to lead a quiet life with marriage and a family of my own and to forget that I should be "King of the Jews" either in a spiritual sense or in a purely material one.

Condition of the World

When I came to teach the truths of my Heavenly Father, the Hebrew nation was struggling under the tyranny of the Roman Empire. The barbarism practiced by the pagan conquerors, in addition to the cruelties evoked by the Hebrew rulers, placed an unrelenting heartless yoke of oppression upon the Jews and their way of life.

The group of Palestinian Jews known as the Pharisees was composed of the common people, the artisans and the tradesmen who were downtrodden by the Sadducees. The Sadducees were the rich and aristocratic priests, the ruling class, an elitist group who cared nothing for the Scriptures except as their own interests were concerned. These two religious parties disagreed frequently over the interpretation of the oral law which was the Hebrew code of unwritten interpretations of the Mosaic law.

The Pharisees were deeply concerned with immortality of the soul inasmuch as their own plight on earth made them seek for justice in an ideal world beyond the grave. They felt that God in His righteousness had of necessity to embrace a kingdom in which justice and mercy would be the established order. That is why the Pharisees were willing to listen to me; yet they were not fully capable of understanding the principles of the Divine Love and the "rebirth" It brings. For some centuries the Pharisees had battled stubbornly against the Sadducees' denial of immortality. The Sadducees had clung to their faith of man's entry into paradise through the keeping of the Ten Commandments and the Torah. In their decrees, precepts and interpretations which stemmed from these holy works, Divine Love was alien to their thoughts and fundamental concepts of religion which prevented them from accepting me as the Messiah.

At this time the world was almost completely devoid of spiritual conception of the true relationship of God to man. God was a being of "power" and "wrath" only. Because of this conception, the Jews were devoid of the knowledge of God's Divine Nature and attributes. They only knew Him as a God who was interested in their material welfare and did not realize that He was a God who wanted them to know Him as their spiritual Father and Saviour from the sinful and evil nature which they

19

had possessed for so long.

When I came, they looked upon me, that is, those who accepted me as their Messiah, as the one who would redeem them from the slavery which their Roman conquerors had placed upon them and make them a great and independent nation more powerful than all the other nations of earth and fit to rule the entire world. This is all wrong and could not happen for God is not the God of any nation or race and, as such, will not help any nation commit acts of aggression to gain victory over another. God, however, will respond to every individual who comes to Him in true supplication seeking His help.

The Jews had no conception of my true mission nor what the Divine Love actually was. The one who had the best approximate knowledge of it was Mary Magdalene through a certain predisposition of her soul. John had a realization of what my coming to earth meant and that was because of the great amount of love that was a part of his nature. My other disciples until shortly before my death looked upon me only as a saviour from their burdens which the Roman yoke had placed upon them. I explained my entire mission to John and taught him the spiritual truths which I had come to teach, that is, the way in which mortals could become immortals.

Hence, only in John's Gospel is it written the necessary requirement for a full redemption and salvation—I mean the declaration—"That you must be born again in order to enter into the kingdom of heaven" (John 3:5). This is the true way by which one can become a child of God and be fit to live in and enjoy the heaven of God's kingdom.

The First Disciples

My first disciples were comparatively ignorant men, fishermen by occupation, who had no education above the ordinary working man of the time. When I called upon them to be my disciples, they were surprised and hesitated. The knowledge they gained during our time together came from their faith in the great truths which I taught them and in their observations of the great power which I displayed and in the great love which I possessed. My first disciples were quite different in their individual personalities but were united with me throughout our travels during my mission in Palestine and were the recipients of my daily instructions, advice and encouragement. Despite all the perplexities and divergences of thoughts, ambition and degrees of faith on the part of my first disciples, I was able to weld them into a very capable group of men devoted to the cause of bringing the kingdom of God to human possession.

Any religious differences among my followers or any disputes of a personal nature were settled by me amicably and not in a formal manner, but rather in an informal manner as befitted the men who followed my teachings. This was done without recourse to the legal and technical formulas presented by the churches of today. My disciples saw that through prayer to God His Love gives humility, forbearance and forgiveness and, if one does this, he will show that the Divine Love is present in his soul. Prayer to God causes Divine Love to flow into the human soul and in time It displaces, or causes to displace, suspicion, judgements, jealousies and competition.

My first disciples needed Divine Love in their souls to have a common bond to provide the way for a relationship of soul between them. At first Peter understood this in a material way and thought I was referring to baptism. However, this was not the case, and so you see, I used water to implement my teachings of the Divine Love in a way my disciples could understand. I also used many other illustrations in addition to water, such as the bread, the new cloth, the new wine or vineyard.

Philip and Nathaniel both proclaimed me to be the Messiah, that is to say, the "Son of God" or the Redeemer. Andrew was the one who told Peter that he had met the Messiah, and thus Peter came to meet me, but he was not first to make this announcement. Peter possessed more love than the other disciples except for John. John was a man of a very affectionate nature and was with me a great deal during my ministry. Although he was not what was called a learned man, he was acquainted with the philosophies of the prophets of the Old Testament. John was selected by me to be one of my disciples because of his susceptibility to my teachings and the great possibility for developing the quality of his love.

Because of his love Peter understood that I was the true Son of the living God (John 6:69), but he never declared that I was God. He was a man filled with zeal and ambition, but his development of love was not sufficient to enable him to realize fully that my kingdom was not to be an earthly one. After my death the conviction of my teachings came to Peter in all their truth and fullness, and he became the most powerful and influential of all my disciples.

Nicodemus

When I was teaching in Palestine, I had a meeting with Nicodemus, the son of Gurion the Pharisee. His father was a rabbi who held religious discussion groups as was the custom of the day. Nicodemus wanted to know about the kingdom of God and how to enter therein. Since he was not able to understand fully my meaning, he came secretly one night to hear from me in private what he had only been able to glimpse at my public sermons in the market place. Nicodemus could not understand the Divine Love or the transformation of the soul from the human into the Divine, so I had recourse then to a parable as I usually had in speaking to the people, "Except a man be born again, he cannot see the kingdom of God" (John 3:3).

He could understand a spiritual "rebirth" only through obedience to the laws of God, the doing of good, the practicing of mercy and charity, righteousness in conduct and pity for the widow and the orphan. In short he understood repentance from evil and a return to God in the prophetic sense of the term, and he thought this gave immortality of the soul. I had to show him that the practicing of these virtues purified the soul and made it a perfect human soul in the eyes of God, but to enter the kingdom, the soul had to be transformed into a Divine soul through God's Divine Nature—Love. To his query I showed that being born of the flesh was the work of the womb, and that in this sense there was no possibility of "rebirth", but spiritually the soul could be reborn into a Divine soul with the transformation taking place as the individual's soul opens through prayer and obtains the Divine Love.

It is this divinity that renders the soul immortal and enables one to see the kingdom of God, not the perfection of the human soul which results from the doing of good works and the practicing of charity and righteousness.

Sermon on the Mount

Not all the sayings and blessings attributed to the Sermon on the Mount were given at once or at one  particular time as is recorded in the Gospel (Matthew 5:2). Instead, they are the result of a great number of sermons dealing with the spiritual lives of the Jews who lived at the time and were put together by the Gospel copyists in the form of a synopsis to cover a considerable vista of spiritual truths. Much of what I said pertained to the development of the human or natural love because this was the only love known to the Jews at the time. It was these sermons which deal with the development of this love as found in the moral code and the exhortations of the Old Testament writings that could best be understood by my hearers and could be used as a bridge which leads to the unknown subject of the Divine Love and the "rebirth" It brings.

In the Gospels there are a number of blessings which I never used at all, and others that were the subjects of considerable sermons rather than the brief blessings as recorded. I did say, "Blessed are the poor in spirit" (Matthew 5:3). By this I meant that those without spirituality, but who realized it, were blessed because this knowledge or intuition of their spiritual lack would turn them to God either to seek His laws and obtain spiritual development in that way or turn to His Divine Love and obtain soul development.

I also blessed the people who listened to me because of their gentleness or meekness for they would inherit the land. By this I meant that violence and quarrels and wars were sinful in the eyes of God and keeping from these offenses would enable mortals to come into harmony and purity to the point of eventually reaching the heaven of purified souls. I taught that gentility of heart could now be obtained through God's Divine Love which would not merely purify the soul but also transform it so that the sins of vengeance, hatred, ambition, murder and bitterness would cease to be encrustations of that soul. The resultant gentility of heart would fit that soul for a wonderful home in the spirit world. This is what I meant by, "The meek shall inherit the earth" (Matthew 5:5). I did not mean the material earth but the promised land of the New Jerusalem; and not for the material body, but for the human soul in its spirit body transformed into a Divine Angel.

I said, "Blessed are they that mourn for they shall be comforted" (Matthew 5:4). What I meant by this was that there would be more than the mere religious consolation for the bereaved who are saddened by the death of a loved one. But to those who have lost loved ones can come the faith that God is our Father and that His spiritual universe is populated with the souls of those who have departed from the earth. These spirits are alive and working out their progress towards such happiness as can never be achieved on earth. The grave simply took their envelope of flesh. So you see, their dear departed are still alive and will be with them again in the future. This was the comfort I spoke of for the Hebrew people who had a very limited understanding of the spiritual aspects of life after death.

I blessed the people saying, "Blessed are the pure in heart for they shall see God" (Matthew 5:8). I did not mean this in a literal way, for this is impossible, but in a spiritual way. What I meant by "the pure in heart" was not merely those who had achieved the paradise of the Hebrews but those who had an understanding of God's existence by their purity of heart in the soul sense—that is, transformed by the Divine Love. Through this Love would come the ability of the soul to see God in all of His Love and beauty. I do not mean that possessors of Divine Love will actually see God (John 1:18) in form or feature, but what I meant was that their soul perceptions would be in such condition that all the attributes of God will appear vividly, so that they will be as real as anything that can be seen with our spirit vision.

Thus, you see, the blessings had a spiritual as well as a soul aspect, and those who could not understand the meaning of the Divine Love could understand the blessings as they pertained to the human or natural love.

Healing

I healed the sick, the deaf, the withered hand of the palsied man and the blind man at the pool of Siloam: he was cured because of his faith (John 9:7). There was also a woman who sought me out to have me cure her sick daughter, and she addressed me as rabbi for she knew I was of the Jewish nation. I told her to approach, although some of my eager disciples wished to chase her away, and it was through her faith that I was able to heal her daughter (Matthew 15:22-23).

Healing is affected as a result of rapport between the mortal doctor or healer and the spirit healers who are transmitting those therapeutic forces and energies to the ailing person. The healers through their spiritual condition can attract the spirit healers; however, if the sick person through faith and prayer can lift himself above the earth plane, the spirit healer can work directly with the patient to accomplish the healing. In either case Divine Love is not necessary, but faith in God that He will help and heal will not only set into motion the healing forces of the spirit world, but will also put the patient in condition by which the evil spirits, who may intensify or cause the distress to persist, are separated from their contact with and control of the patient to allow the healers to do their work. All the ministering Angels who do this work were once inhabitants of a physical body and, as such, have the sympathy and love which enables them to understand the sufferings of humans.

The prayers and faith of a loved one for a sick person are of great benefit. Often the best physicians are those who, in earnestness of love and sympathy, send their prayers to God in faith that He will accomplish what mortal medicine cannot. Although there are times when, despite prayer, the death of a loved one does occur. This is due to aside from the spiritual forces engaged, the healing process depends upon the condition of the organ to be restored. An organ which is in good functioning order can be restored to perfect health regardless of the pathological disturbance from which it may suffer. But, an organ that has reached a condition of irreversible weakness or malfunction through abuse, misuse or old age cannot be healed or restored. Deterioration of the body is normal due to aging, then the time comes for that person to relinquish its tired worn out body and enter upon a new life in its spirit body.

In all my performances of healings or in any of my teachings I never did or said anything which worked against any human being.

Lazarus

I wish to explain my visit to the house of Lazarus and my healing him of his unconscious state which was actually a coma that was not known to people of the time. His condition has been erroneously described as death by the Gospel copyists. They were wrong in this for I did not say, "This sickness is not unto death but, for the glory of God that the Son of Man might be glorified" (John 11:4), for this meant that the sickness would not end in death only because I might be glorified by raising him from the dead. Instead, what I did say was, "This sickness is not unto death, for through the power of God, the "Son of God" will heal and be glorified." What this meant was that I would show that I had been sent by God to cure Lazarus of his illness.

Furthermore, I did say as recorded, "Our friend Lazarus sleepeth; but I go, that I may awaken him out of his sleep" (John 11:11). Now, the Gospel of John, which at this point was not written by John, declares that by "sleep" I meant death, but this is not true for had I meant that Lazarus was dead, I would have used one of the expressions which were commonly used at the time to indicate death. These were "to sleep with one's Father" or "to sleep in the dust" or "to sleep in perpetual sleep." Hence, when I said, "Lazarus was asleep," I meant that he was in that unconscious state in which one is dying in sleep. When I wept, and this is true for I did weep (John 11:35), it was because I was touched by my emotions of love for him.

I also wish to explain an expression which, if not correctly understood, tends to give an impression of cruelty and indifference to human suffering in my teachings. I never advocated or taught mutilation of the body in any form such as the saying attributed to me in the Gospels, "If thy right eye offend thee, pluck it out and cast it from thee for it is profitable for thee that one of thy members should perish and not that thy whole body be cast into hell" (Matthew 5:29). This does not give the true meaning of my saying for I meant that the eye reflects the state of the soul, the seat of the emotions, so that if the eye reveals a wicked emotion, it means the soul is possessed of a wicked emotion and, by plucking out the wicked eye, I simply meant to pluck out the evil emotion from the soul.

In the same way my reference to the cutting off the hand that offends (Matthew 5:30) did not mean to refer literally to the physical hand, but to the action performed by the hand resulting from a sinful soul. I simply meant eradication of the evil emotion in the soul that produced an evil action. The physical plucking out of an eye or the cutting off of a limb could have no effect on the body to free it from sin, for it is not the body but the soul that is sinful; the body simply carries out the desires of the soul. Such mutilations could not have any effect upon the soul in the way of eliminating sin; for sin is eliminated through will power, prayer for the Father's Love and through that change in the soul's condition which causes man to turn to God in the earnestness of prayer to seek forgiveness.

Transfiguration

At the time of my birth, Divine Love was bestowed to mortals and spirits alike. Once spirits living in the higher realms came to know of this gift and began to seek for It and receive It, they became pure and holy spirits free from sin and error and partakers of the Divine Essence of God and possessors of immortality.

Thus, at the time of the Transfiguration on the Mount, Moses and Elijah were the leaders of this group of spirits who had understood and had obtained some of this Divine Love. The appearance of the three of us together on the Mount was to show that Divine Love had been bestowed by the Heavenly Father and received by myself and those deserving spirits. Moses and Elijah had this

Love to such a degree that they were shining and bright. When Peter, John and James accompanied me to the Mount and witnessed the event, they fell to their faces because of the exceeding brightness of our countenance. The voice they heard saying "Hear ye him," which proclaimed that I was the well-beloved son (Luke 9:35) was not the voice of God, but one of the Divine spirits whose mission it was to make this proclamation.

I never said, "but I say unto you Elijah is come" (Matthew 17:12). What I did say was "but I say unto you that one like Elijah has come," for I did refer to John the Baptist who, in his type of sermon, his temperament, and even his garb and food, was a throwback to Elijah. Here the similarity ended for each of these men lived different lives and are individual spirits both living in the kingdom of God at the same time.

Greater Works

"Verily, verily, I say unto you, he that believeth in me, the works that I do shall he do also and greater works than these shall he do, because I go unto my Father" (John 14:12). What I meant by "works" are those works which the world considered as miracles. I assured my disciples that they would have the power to do similar works or perform similar miracles and to a greater extent than I had performed them (John 14:12), "greater" referred to quantity not quality. This power, or the successful exercise of it, was not dependent upon belief in my name, but upon their faith in the power of God, and in the fact that

He would confer that power upon them. There is no virtue in my name or in me as the individual Jesus, but all virtue rests in the faith that they might have in the Father. I never performed any of the miracles on my own, they were all performed by God working through me (John 5:19). Just as He worked through me, He would work through my disciples who acquired the necessary faith.

The Bible expression, "And whatsoever ye shall ask in my name, that will I do, that the Father may be glorified in the Son" (John 14:13), the belief that my name is sufficient to cause the workings of miracles is all wrong. I never said that such belief was what was required. Neither did I say, "Whatsoever should be asked of the Father in my name would be given to men" (John 15:16). I am not a part of the Godhead and my name does not have any miraculous influence with God. I am a man as other men were men, only I had become filled with the Divine Love of God which made me at-one with Him. Thus, I had knowledge of His laws that enabled me to bring into operation those forces which would cause the desired effects to appear as realities. Belief in my name caused no working of these laws or the response of God to any supplications.

All acts which are apparently miracles are controlled by laws just as those things which mortals call the workings of nature are controlled by laws. When sufficient faith is acquired, there comes to its possessor a knowledge of these laws. It may not be, as you would say, a knowledge or consciousness that is perceptible to the ordinary physical senses, but instead is perceptible to that inner sense of the soul which is the one that enables comprehension of the things of the spirit. With the knowledge of the inner sense people may control these laws so that those effects which they bring about seem to be contrary to the accustomed workings of the laws of nature and appear to be as miracles. Until my disciples had acquired the faith that brought this knowledge to their inner sense, they could not perform any miracles.

Miracles

At the marriage feast at Cana (John 2:1), an alleged miracle that needs clarification, is my supposed changing of water to wine. A cousin of mine on my mother's side of the family was being married and, as the wine ran out, I was able to procure some from a nearby wine dealer by simply paying for it, and I used water jugs to bring it back to the wedding party. This New Testament story was borrowed from the Greek account of Dionysius of Elis, the god of wine who would make jars of water turn to wine overnight by putting them into a concealed chamber.

When news arrived of my cousin John's death, I retreated to a remote place in the hills of Trans-Jordan to pray. When I came out, I was met by a great multitude of people and was moved with compassion for them and healed their sick. It was getting late and the people were hungry. Those who ate supper with me had bread and fish and wine (Matthew 14:17), and we even had figs and dates which the New Testament does not mention. I  did not create this food in some miraculous way even though I had wonderful powers and understood the workings of the spiritual laws to a far greater extent than any mortal who had ever lived. Despite this I had not the power to increase the loaves and fishes as is set forth in the account of the miracle. To be able to do so would be against the laws of God which govern the material things of His creation and beyond the powers conferred on any mortal or spirit. The food had either been brought along  by the people or, in the case of the fish, they had been caught by my disciples. However, I did tell them where to cast their nets to be able to make a great haul of fish (John 21:6) which they did, and this took place as a result of my psychic knowledge that a large school of fish had just reached that area of the lake. In the Book of Kings II, the story in which Elisha feeds one hundred men with

31

only the first fruits of some corn and bread (2 Kings 4:42) is an incident which the New Testament writers adopted to misrepresent me to have fed five thousand.

That evening my disciples took their fishing boat and turned back to Galilee in the vicinity of Capernaum. I remained behind to dismiss the multitude which was not four or five thousand but considerably less, and then I withdrew to pray. Later I took one of the little boats of the many which were anchored near the shore and made my way in it that night. As the wind was strong, I was able to catch up with my disciples who were happy to see me and took me into their boat. The sea was rough and they were frightened (Matthew 14:24), Peter told me to stand up by  the mast so the men could see me and gain faith and courage. The moonlight was shining on my white robe and it appeared, as they told me later, that I looked like a ghost and from the shore it seemed as though I was walking on the waves (Matthew 14:26). The latter New Testament writers turned to tales in Greek mythology regarding this miracle, and in a similar way they read that Poseidon, the god of the sea, walked on water, and this was sufficient for their imaginations to have me also walk on water.

Now regarding my casting out evil spirits, the incident of the swine was not recorded accurately. I had no authority to permit the evil spirits to enter into the swine. The result of such a happening would be that the property of the innocent owner would have been taken from him and lost. This would not have been in consonance with my love and ideas of what was just to allow the swine to receive these spirits and thereby perish (Matthew 8:31-32).

All of the instances of alleged miracles which were attributed to me were not done with any maliciousness of heart but with the obvious desire to stress my supernatural powers to the point of making me a divinity equal to that of God as part of their desire to institutionalize Christianity. Those in power wished to keep that power by making the priestly order and its functions the dominant part of the religion. In this way the Church eventually fell into the same pit of ambition and worldliness which the early Church had accused the Sadducees and Hebrew religious leaders of doing.

This perpetuated a system entirely man-made which lacked in the essential of spirituality, the Divine Love of God for humanity which was the paramount reason for my ministry and the cornerstone of my teachings.

The Good Shepherd

As I said when on earth, "He that enters into the sheepfold in any other way than through the gate is a thief  and a robber" (John 10:1), and is not fitted for the kingdom. I never said that I was the Good Shepherd for that referred to my Heavenly Father. This statement (John 10:11) was inserted many years after my death in order to raise me up equal to God. Instead, what I said was that the Father is the Good Shepherd and the sheepfold is the kingdom of heaven. I was the door through which the sheep came into the sheepfold and into the presence and knowledge of the Shepherd or the Porter who opens the door and is the Father. The Father gives eternal life to His sheep, and I am the way, the door, through which the sheep may enter the sheepfold of eternal life (John 10:7). In the Psalms it was pointed out that the Good Shepherd, God, would use King David, or better said, a root of David as a helper to bring the sheep into the fold.

One of the best known Psalms is the twenty-third written by David which I used in my teachings to show the distinction between the old teachings and those which

I gave to the people as part of my mission. In this Psalm, God is described as a Shepherd who leads His flock beside the still waters and to lie down in green pastures (Psalms 23:2). This Psalm can be interpreted first as nostalgia for the countryside and its tranquility away from the cares and vexations of city life and second it means longing to be alone with God's creations to have a chance to shed from one's soul the crassness of the earth plane and its activities and, in the retreat to nature, commune with God and purify one's heart. This Psalm has a more spiritual interpretation and is really a description of the kingdom of heaven for such things are there to make the soul happy in its celestial home.

Here the Psalm gives to the people an understanding that death does not mean the cessation of the conscious personality of the soul for the Psalm mentions, "Yea, though I pass through the valley of the shadow of death, I shall fear no evil for Thou art with me; Thy rod and Thy staff, they comfort me" (Psalms 23:4). This picture, which the people could understand really meant, that God's messengers would care for the troubled soul entering the spirit world, and that faith in God would enable His ministering Angels to help that soul to progress to a point where it would eventually find the peace and happiness of · the still waters and the green pastures. This Psalm describes this by means of the Father's feast for the soul; "Thou preparest a table before me in the presence of mine enemies; thou anointest my head with oil; my cup runneth over" (Psalms 23:5). Here I expressed that the soul with the Divine Love in it eliminates all thoughts of vengeance, or overcoming enemies, and entertains only sentiments of love for its fellow souls.

When I quoted the Psalm, "And I shall dwell in the house of the Lord forever" (Psalms 23:6), I simply meant that life in the paradise of the Hebrews has no certainty of immortality, whereas the soul possessed of the Divine Love has a consciousness of its immortality and of its existence for all eternity. I used many Psalms and other passages in the Old Testament writings to show the greater glory that comes to the possessor of God's Divine Love.

THE LAST WEEK

Entry into Jerusalem

Isaiah was positive that the Father's word must come from Jerusalem (Isaiah 2:3). I believed this and that is the reason I went to Jerusalem to bring the message of the Father's Love to the city of David. When my disciples and I approached Jerusalem at Bethphage near the Mount of Olives, I sent two of them ahead telling them to go to the village visible in the distance and bring to me the ass and her colt which they would find tied there. "If anyone questions why you want them, explain that they are for your Master who needs them for the Lord's work, and they will let you take them" (Matthew 21:2-3). This was the fulfillment of the prophecy, "Behold, Jerusalem! Your king will come riding humbly on a colt, the foal of an ass!" (Zechariah 9:9). My disciples went forth and carried out my instructions. They returned with the animals and put cloaks over their backs and I got upon the colt. When I entered the city, many people put their cloaks on the road while others cut palm branches and laid them along the path. The crowd that preceded me and those who followed praised me saying; "God bless the descendent of David, he who comes in the name of the Lord" (Matthew 21:9). The people were excited, some asked who I was, others answered, "This is the Savior, the promised Messiah, Jesus of Nazareth" (Matthew 21:11).

Zechariah saw that the Messiah to come must be a

human being possessed of the transcendental spiritual qualities of love and humility. In addition, he saw that the Messiah of God would not only have Israel at heart but all nations and would bring peace to the war-torn world through his care, his love and his mercy. I was very much impressed by the verses of Zechariah, and the Divine Love dwelling in my soul told me that this concept of the Messiah was in accord with what God had willed for His "Christ". So when I set out for Jerusalem, I chose to enter the city exactly in the manner described by Zechariah.

Cleansing of the Temple

Upon seeing the merchants in the Temple courtyard, I said to them "God's house shall be called the house of prayer; but ye have made it a den of thieves" (Matthew 21:13). I entered with a piece of rope in which I had tied knots and, as I swung it about, the animals in the courtyard of which there were many to be sold as sacrifice for the Passover stampeded, which overturned the tables and scattered the wares. Afterwards, I healed the blind and lame who came to me at the Temple.

The sacrifice of animals performed by the priests was a pagan concept and practice which Abraham, enlightened by God, had abandoned. However, it was consistent with the priesthood's plan to perform religious functions of a special or national nature. These sacrifices enabled the priesthood to live for they had difficulties in making ends meet because the people were not so generous in their contributions towards them.

The story of Abraham binding his son, Isaac, to an altar, and the latter's being saved by an angel of God from sacrifice at the hand of his father (Genesis 22:9) is not, therefore, a narrative depicting the true test of Abraham's faith in God as Bible commentators so erroneously think. Abraham's faith in God had been put to the test again and again by the rigors and hardships which he had faced and borne for months and months in the slow and exhausting trek from his native Ur to begin, at his old age, a new life at the call of a God he could not see but whom he knew in his heart was the living King of the universe. The saving of Isaac, then, was not a test at all, but the undeniable proof stamped with the authority of God Himself who demanded true worship in obedience to His statutes of righteousness, justice and mercy.

Some of the Pharisees came to me with a woman taken in adultery. They came to test my judgement to see in what way my decision would differ from that of Moses. The New Testament states, "This they said, tempting him, that they might have something with which to accuse him" (John 8:6). If I had declared against stoning, they would accuse me of breaking the Mosaic law, and if I had upheld the Mosaic law, they were going to accuse me of inhumanity inconsistent with the Divine forgiveness of God and a brutal imposter. The Gospel of John does not mention their motives, but I knew what was in their minds and I made my decision as John recorded it, "He that is without sin among you, let him first cast a stone at her" (John 8:7).

I left Jerusalem and went to the city of Bethany and lodged there for the night (Matthew 21:17).

Fig Tree

When I returned to Jerusalem, it was Monday of the Passion week. I had come from the house of Lazarus where I had enjoyed a good breakfast prepared by Mary and served to me by Martha. I know that in the Gospels of Matthew and Mark they state that because I was hungry I stopped at a fig tree, but when I found no fruit I cursed the tree which, according to the Gospel, immediately withered (Matthew 21:19).

What actually happened was that when I came upon the fig tree I was not hungry but merely curious because it was not time for fig trees to give fruit, and seeing leaves on the tree, I thought I may also see fruit. My disappointment did not cause me to curse the tree. As a matter of fact I never cursed anything or anyone in my entire life. The tree did not miraculously begin to wither and it was not Matthew who wrote those words but another who, many years later, was interested in showing my divinity through the only way he could understand my messiahship—supernatural powers rather than soul development.

Taught at the Temple

When I preached in Palestine to the crowds and also to the Jewish leaders, I taught the fulfillment of the prophecies. I had discussions with opponents of the elastic concept of law and some of these were Pharisees who argued not in the vicious or venomous vein that one reads in the New Testament (Matthew 23:29), but in the atmosphere that so often prevails where the views held are important and precious to each. I never sought to provoke the high priests by adapting a hostile attitude toward them but urged them to believe that God's Love was available as it had been promised to the Jewish nation through the word of the old prophets.

Before my death I taught at the Temple at Jerusalem (John 7:14). I was very much aware of the evils found among the Hebrew priesthood, and I was also convinced through my studies of the prophets of old and the teachings I received direct from God that the priesthood was not essential to a religion calling for a direct relationship between the human soul and the Soul of the Heavenly Father through Divine Love. It was not my intention to harm or destroy the prevailing system which had been built up through the centuries to perpetuate the priesthood as an integral part of the organization of the

Hebrew people whether Israel, Judah or both. The Hebrew nation had been established as one consecrated to the Almighty with the priesthood as the intermediary between God and the people. The priesthood were to be the leaders of a people designated to be a light to the gentiles (Luke 2:32) and who would eventually lead the pagan peoples to the path of true belief and worship of the eternal God.

This was my first opportunity to present my claims as Messiah before the chief priests and rulers and most learned amongst the Hebrew people in matters pertaining to religion. I made known that my mission was to proclaim the New Covenant (Hebrews 8:13) between the Heavenly Father and the people of Israel and that the Divine Love was now present and could be obtained by all who might seek It through the earnest longing of their souls. I was the visible sign of Its presence for in my soul reposed the Divine Love, the Nature and Essence of God.

To the Hebrew rulers, my claims appeared false for it had been prophesied that no one would know from whence the Messiah would come (John 7:27), whereas I was well known as being Jesus of Nazareth. They also knew my father, Joseph, and that he, too, came from Bethlehem. They deemed a man not to be of his native town but of the one in which he had lived most of his life and was associated. Thus, Jerusalem was considered the city of the great King David rather than Bethlehem where he was born. This type of argument showed a recourse to technicalities in the determination of the priests not to recognize me as the Messiah for they felt this would upset their high position as the religious leaders of the nation which they were unwilling to relinquish.

I replied to their minute scriptural objections on their own terms by proclaiming that it was not true that they knew where I was from or who my father was. For they referred to Joseph as my father whom they knew well, but I was referring to God, my Heavenly Father, whom they did not know (John 8:19). Neither did they know from whence I came as a Divine soul, nor how or when I was created. The references of the rabbis to my father, Joseph, were later eliminated from the Gospels for mention of my earthly parents was a thorn in the side of the later revisionists who labored zealously to make of me a god-man born of a virgin and second person of a supposed trinity which of course has no foundation in fact.

These technicalities were a subterfuge and a manner of debating issues which were dear to their hearts by laying emphasis on hair-splitting intellectual distinctions which resulted from subtle interpretations of the law which were foreign to real basic issues and spiritual insight achieved through soul-seeking to know the truth. When I quoted from Isaiah, as the Hebrew leaders did, I stated that the Father had said, "Incline your ear and come unto me, hear, and your soul shall live and I will make a Covenant with you even as the sure mercies of David. Behold, I have given him as a witness to the people, a leader and commander to the people" (Isaiah 55:3-4). This was known to all who received instruction concerning Jehovah so that they knew He had appointed a Messiah over them in a descendant of David. Hence, they should accept me as their Messiah, inasmuch as I had indeed come to enable their souls to live by making available to them the gift of immortality through the Father's Love accompanied by the power of healing which I performed to attest to the truth of my mission.

I further informed the priests that if they wished to ascertain the truth of my words, they should test my teachings that Divine Love was now available and to pray for It in earnest. If you do this in sincerity, this Love, conveyed through the Holy Spirit, would burn and glow in your souls by which sign you would realize that It was present therein.

I also stated that these teachings were not mine but those of my Heavenly Father who had commanded me to proclaim them to the children of Israel, and that having been sent by Him, I could do nothing of my own (John

8:28). What power I had, I received directly from God and I did not say that I could do what I saw the Father do, or imitate Him (John 5:19), as the Gospel states, for that would give me power equal to that of the Father which would be blasphemy. No mortal or spirit will ever through all eternity have power equal to that of the Almighty, the creator of the physical and spiritual universes. This revision was added many years later.

Last Supper

The first holiday of the Sacred Year is Passover, the seventh month of the year, which begins at sundown of

the 14th of Nissan and continues through the 15th and 16th (March-April). It celebrated the deliverence of the Hebrews from slavery in

Egypt by Moses and required the presence of every male over twelve years of age before the sanctuary of the Lord.

The Passover Festival is many sided, from brief Spiritualism with the invisible appearance of the prophet Elijah to mystic messianism, and references to the Afikoman, the broken matzah, but it is essentially national and patriotic. Except for a certain break that took place several hundreds of years before my birth, Hebrews have gathered together to tell of this great march to freedom and the Lord's protection from Pharaoh's army whose chariots and soldiers perished in the rising tides of the Nile (Sea of Reeds). This safe Exodus was so extraordinary in nature that Hebrews of all ages and times are commanded to feel as though this delivery had been done unto them personally. Annual instruction is given to the young illustrated by history and embellished by tradition. This is the festival of Liberty I loved and observed faithfully during my life, and it was during this festival I chose to return to Jerusalem where I met death in the execution of my mission as the Messiah of God.

When my disciples and I went to celebrate the Passover at Jerusalem, I remained near Bethany. I did not go up to the feast because I feared trouble with the Jewish authorities. I switched my plans to go to Jerusalem to a time when I was least expected (John 7:10), and would thus be able to make my appearance and teach there without being stopped by the Jews or cause a disturbance between them and my disciples. I knew that once I was in the city, the authorities would not dare to molest me.

My parents went on to Jerusalem to arrange for the preparation of the Upper Room. Since my coming was fraught with danger, it was decided that Peter and John would make known our readiness to come to the Upper Room by meeting a young man with a pitcher near the Kedron stream, and he would take us there for the occasion (Mark 14:13). While it was not mentioned in the Gospels and many have conjectured as to the identity of this person with the pitcher, I should like to inform you that he was the writer of a Gospel and his name was John Mark.

In the evening I joined my disciples and just before we began the Passover meal, I said to Peter, "If I wash thee not, thou hast no part of me" (John 13:8), but Peter objected to this ablution. My purpose in this was to use the word and ceremony of washing not as a natural cleansing of the body nor even a symbol of the spiritual cleansing with baptism. I meant to use the word "washing" as a washing from sin, and I had to do this in order to make my teachings concrete and something my disciples could see and understand.

I told them, "If ye love me, you will keep my Commandment that ye love one another even as I have loved you" (John 15:12). This was the Eleventh Commandment and was above the Ten Commandments of Moses. It was the law of Love, and it was obedience to this Commandment which would bring what is called the "Comforter." I wanted them not merely to love one another but all humanity, for "one another" was a term which meant not only for the circle of disciples, but for all people. This was the only Commandment I gave to my disciples and no other. I never said in teaching my disciples the Lord's prayer that they should pray that God would not lead them into temptation.

I said be thankful for your daily bread, but I never said that my flesh or my blood should be consumed in order for my followers to attain salvation (John 6:54). The conception that the wine and bread was my blood and body was not a Hebrew one, but was very popular and practiced among the Greeks. The cult of Dionysius, Orpheus, Isis and others sacrificed animals to the gods and ate their flesh  and drank their blood under the impression or illusion that in this mystical rite the animal sacrificed represented the god. Thus by eating the animal's flesh and drinking its blood the devote became at-one, at least temporarily, with the god himself. These Greek ideas together with others found their way into the Christian ceremonies. The concept of the transubstantiation of the blood and flesh came from the pagan rite and was adopted for the deification of me as the "Son of God". Thus, the combination of elements that comprise the Eucharist was given the stamp of authenticity by the Greek writers of the Second Century.

I do not want to be remembered for the tragedy on the cross which was only the result of the malice and envy of the Jews, and the blood spilt is not an element that enters into God's "plan of redemption". Besides, with this sacrament there is always more or less the worshipping of me as God which is erroneous and an act which I deplore. I do not want men to believe that they can be saved by any sacrifice on my part or by any blood which I may have shed as a result of my crucifixion.

As a matter of fact I told my disciples that, "The two greatest truths are; God is Love and you must be born again" (John 3:7). Then you will find as you are transformed by the Divine Love that you will, by your very nature, follow all the other Commandants. You will love your neighbor as yourself and, seeking first the kingdom of God, all else will be added unto you (Matthew 6:33). The New Covenant of the Heart prophesied by Ezekiel and Jeremiah (Jeremiah 30:31-33) is the transforming Grace of God's Love and is available to all who should seek to obtain It through prayer. I have shown the way to receive It, the Living Waters from the Fountainhead of the Father's Infinite Love.

Betrayal and Arrest

My mission was not imposed upon me, but shall I say I imposed it upon myself because I had to be true to myself and faithful to my Heavenly Father who had sent me to declare the "Glad Tidings" of the "New Heart" (Ezekiel 18:31). The day preceding my arrest I taught in the vicinity of the Temple, and it thundered so that some of the people who were listening to my discourse thought that an angel, or God, had spoken to me. The weather was cold for, as it is recorded in the New Testament, Peter had to warm his hands in the courtyard of the high priests (John 18:18). It was not in April that I was arrested and put to death, but it occurred in March.

I understood that my mission had to continue regardless of the threats against my life made by the Jews. I knew there was danger and the possible consequences, but I expected to be able to escape and I would have had it not been for the impulsiveness of my youngest and most impetuous disciple, Judas. I never taught that my death on the cross was ordained by God nor that Judas should betray me. In fact, my death was never a part of that which God considered necessary in the performance of my mission. Although it was certain that I would die, the manner of my death was not foreordained as written (Matthew 20:19). I never told any of my brothers and sisters, as it is recorded in the New Testament, that my time had not yet come while their time was opportune, always (John 7:6). For that would mean that I had an understanding of the time when I should be arrested and handed over to the Roman authorities for execution, and I should like to emphasize that I did not know when my time would come.

Judas was impatient with the people's slowness to learn the truths which I had come to teach, so he went to the chief priests and told them he would help them capture me. The thirty pieces of silver they offered him was incidental for his desire was for me to show them my power. Judas was so convinced of my sonship to God that he believed a legion of angels would come in all their glory to protect me from harm. I did not know beforehand that Judas would betray me, and  I never said, "All of you are not clean" (John 13:11), referring to Judas for I did not suspect him of any treachery and, as a matter of fact, when he did betray me, I was taken by surprise.

Because I had been arrested instead of overpowering the authorities, Judas regretted his impetuous actions. He took the thirty pieces of silver back to the chief priests saying, "I only wanted you to recognize the importance of my Master." They told him that why he did it was of no concern to them for now they had me where they wanted me. Judas threw the pieces of silver at their feet and, feeling remorseful beyond endurance, went off and hung himself. The priests took up the silver and, as they looked upon it as blood money, they did not want it in the treasury. After consultation they decided to buy a field of clay for burying strangers known as Potter's Field (Matthew 27:3-7).

Judas was not a bad man as he has been depicted. His betrayal (as it is called) was not for silver or the purpose of gratifying any avarice or because of any jealousy or desire to revenge a wrong, but it was because he was impulsive and had such belief in my powers and my ability to overcome the Jewish leaders in their fight to defeat the objects of my mission. He thought he would be doing me and the cause a great benefit by having it demonstrated to these Jews that I could not be silenced or harmed by any act of theirs. It was really an act that grew out of his love for me and belief in the greatness of my powers. Judas was the youngest of my disciples and was not so easily controlled in his impulses and acts as he would have been had he been older.

At my arrest by the hirelings of the high priests in the Garden of Gethsemane it is mentioned in the New Testament that a youth who was present at the time of my betrayal was seized and that he had to tear himself away from the clutches of the hirelings. In the process he lost his outer garment of linen which left him stripped, but he subsequently escaped (Mark 14:51-52). The Apostle who originally wrote this statement was Mark, and the name of this youth was James who was my younger brother, known as "the lesser". The reason why the hirelings seized James was because he resembled me so much in face and figure that sometimes he was mistaken for me. Some of the hirelings thought that he was really I and that I was really he, and so they sought to arrest him to make certain that they had apprehended the right man.

My brother loved me very much and had begun to believe in my mission to the extent of his capabilities. He followed me when I was arrested, his heart breaking with grief and anxiety. The copyists of the original Gospel of Mark eliminated the name of my brother and inserted the words and a "certain youth" (Mark 14:51) because they did not want to use the word "brother" for it denoted what is really a fact, that my mother was the mother of seven children in the flesh besides myself. The writer also sought to enhance my prestige with readers of the New Testament by showing them to what a great degree I was able to inspire the love and loyalty of a stranger.

It is not true that in the garden Peter nor any one of my

followers with a sword cut off the ear of Malchus (Matthew 26:51), a servant of the high priests, because Peter did not wear a sword but merely a fishing knife. Furthermore, a hostile blow might have meant that the hirelings and servants of the priests might retaliate and club our followers unmercifully as a consequence, a fact which Peter knew as we all did at the time.

The Trial

In those latter days men had appeared and claimed to be specially anointed by God with missions to perform. They were able to gather around them people whom they

impressed with their character and the truth of their teachings. For a short time then they were permitted to declare their claims and doctrines and then were suddenly brought to death by the decree of those who were in authority. These men have long been forgotten and their doctrines have disappeared from memory and only in the instance of my death have I been remembered through the ages.

My trial by the body of men known as the Sanhedrin was in accordance to a rudimentary decree with the Sadducean laws. The Sadducees were aggravated and incensed at the thought that any mortal could call himself the "Son of God". Not in merely the sense that all human beings are the sons and daughters of God, but in that I stated—that I was in the Father and the Father was in me (John 14:10). This seemed to the Jews to be blasphemy because it was putting me on an equal level with God. They felt that such blasphemy destroyed the meaning of God to the Hebrew people and deserved death.

I was accused of breaking the Mosaic law when I healed on the Sabbath (Matthew 12:10). I had even helped a mule out of a hole on that day. However, I did not break the law for restoring the body is far more important than the Sabbath. I contended, to the consternation of those who set their store by rigid rules, that the Sabbath was made for man and not man for the Sabbath (Mark 2:27). This meant that by putting life first as God intended I was not going outside Hebrew law or even bringing a new God-given revelation to mankind, but was following and agreeing with the insight of Haggai, prime mover in the rebuilding of the Temple (Haggai 1:8) and Hebrew prophet par excellence.

The Sadducees had a deep religious conviction and a sense of obligation to protect and keep whole the divine doctrines and teachings of the faith. I stood in the position to them and their religion as a breeder of sedition, they saw me as an enemy and would-be destroyer of the doctrines of the Israelite nation and a seducer of the people. They considered me importunate to the Hebrew religion and a source of potential danger to their harmony with the Roman authorities. It was the spring of the year 29 A.D. I was thirty-six years old. They were willing to accept unfair means through perjured witnesses (Matthew 26:59) in order to eliminate me. They found me guilty of blasphemy and iconoclastic teachings against the beliefs of the Hebrew faith. I appeared not only guilty of treason to their national life but also to the higher God-given life of their religious government.

My father, Joseph, was present at my unfair trial and watched me buffeted and condemned (Mark 14:65). There is evidence in the New Testament to show that nine months before the crucifixion he was alive when I was preaching in Capernaum. The Jews asked each other, "Is not he the son of Joseph and Mary whom we know?" (John 6:42). This shows that they referred to my father as still living at the time.

My father was sick at heart at the treatment I received and at the confirmation of his worst fears. His eyes were opened to the stagnant state of the Sanhedrin at the time, and he realized that what they considered religion was merely farce. He also realized the enormous gulf between their religion as practiced by its most august body and what I proposed in its place—not only to restore its pristine purity and authority, but also to impart its culminating sublimity and grandeur. From the shame and humiliation which my father suffered at seeing his first-born son condemned and executed as a criminal there was born in him the conviction of his son's innocence and the righteousness of his cause and the truth of his mission.

I went to my death, not so I could be a willing sacrifice in a bloody ritual condemned by a "wrathful" exacting God, but because I was faithful to my Heavenly Father and refused to recant or deny my mission that I was the Christ, possessor of the Father's Love and Nature and that I had been sent by Him to teach man the way to His Love and blessings. The great element of tragedy in all this was that the Jews were so mistaken and failed to recognize and accept me as their long looked for Messiah and Deliverer, not from their material condition of bondage, but from the bondage of sin and error in which they had lived for so long.

The act of the Jews to cause my death has been called the great crime of the world and has caused the people themselves to be hated and destroyed as a nation and scattered to all points of the earth. If the people of my nation had received me and accepted and followed my teachings, they would not have become the scattered and persecuted race that they have been all these centuries.

Jurisdiction

The Jewish court was not permitted by their Roman overlords to carry out their sentence, so after I was beaten, they sent me to the Roman Procurator (Pilate) with the accusation that I was attempting to cause a revolution against Caesar by claiming myself "King of the Jews". Pilate arrested me, then he sent me to Herod Antipas (Luke 23:7) who happened to be in Jerusalem at the time to observe the festivities of the Jewish Passover.

Sometime before, Pilate had ordered a number of Galileans to be killed, and this caused enmity between Pilate and Herod who claimed that Pilate had no authority to execute the men since as Galileans they were under his (Herod's) jurisdiction. This coolness was patched up on the occasion of my arrest for Pilate used this opportunity to send me to Herod to ascertain whether or not I was under his jurisdiction as a Galilean. When Herod, through inquiry, discovered that I was born in Bethlehem in Judea and not Galilee, he returned me to Pilate and was pleased that Pilate had extended him the courtesy of consulting him to establish under whose jurisdiction my condemnation and punishment was to be meted out. This is the explanation for the healing of the breach between Pilate and Herod (Luke 23:12) and the reason for the latter's appearance on the scene at the time of my arrest.

The Crucifixion

After my trial I was beaten by Roman soldiers and taken for crucifixion. I was accompanied on my weary march to the cross by a great host of

spirits in whom was vested the most wonderful powers of the spirit world who were all trying to sustain me. At the scene of the crucifixion it grew dark and cloudy, and there were many who thought that this darkness was an indication of God's "anger" at the deed. The fact is that God is Love, and His Love was open even to those who were responsible for my death. God did not express anger because there is no anger in Him, and the storm that darkened that day over Jerusalem simply obeyed the natural order of a new-settled spring for that time of the year.

There was no great concourse of people because many

of my followers stayed away because of fear. There were soldiers and a large number of the members of the Jewish Sanhedrin and a few of my followers present to witness my execution. While I was on the cross, there was no sudden breaking up of nature or of material things, and I did no talking because of the pain and exhaustion of my battered body. Nevertheless, any words that I could have uttered could not have been heard by any followers present because they were kept away from the immediate scene of the execution. The nails that pierced my flesh were hammered into my wrists and not the palms as has been widely believed. Physical death came to me through asphyxiation due to the unnatural position of my body dragging on my outstretched arms on the cross. The rite for the dying was administered to me and, after I had been pronounced dead, my followers were permitted to approach my body and remove it from the cross.

I died without fear for a burning in my soul constantly told me that I could die only in the flesh and that I would retain my consciousness and identity after my passing. Not once during that time did I loose faith in my Heavenly Father or in the truth of my mission. I never voiced any complaints or doubted that God was with me, nor did I call upon Him for help to cause the bitter cup to pass from me (Matthew 26:39), but I did ask Him whether I had done all that I could in the short time of my ministry.

I never said the words which I am supposed to have uttered, "My God, my God, why have you forsaken me?" (Matthew 27:46). This is the first sentence, or opening line, of the twenty-second Psalm which is indeed Messianic in nature for it deals with the suffering of the afflicted. I did not say these words in order to fulfill the prophecy embodied in that Psalm, nor did I say what are supposed to be my last words on earth, "Into thy hands I commend my spirit" (Psalms 31:5), in order to fulfill the saying contained in the old Scriptures for I never said any of these words or sayings. The truth of the matter is that after my death, the copyists who searched the Scriptures found this passage within the Psalms and, therefore, decided that I must have said it. Thus, they wrote the account of my crucifixion with additions in order to show that I had done or said things which would fulfill the Scriptures.

It is true that there were two others who were crucified with me. They were also considered violators of the law and were to be punished by hanging on the cross. I was between them but they did not talk to me. Neither did one mock me nor did the other seek to be converted or ask me to pardon him. I did not tell him that he would be in paradise with me (Luke 23:43) for that was a boon that I could not grant. I had no authority to forgive sin as it is stated in various passages of the New Testament (Luke 5:24) for their places in the world of spirits would not depend upon me, but upon the condition of their souls as the result of their thoughts and deeds while on earth.

The Roman Centurion who officiated at the crucifixion was deeply convinced of my innocence, but he did not say I was the "Son of God" (Mark 15:39) because he did not understand that concept. Yet he did state that he believed in my innocence and, at the Pentecost with the preaching of my disciples and his being convinced that I was resurrected, he converted to Christianity as did some others of the Roman soldiery.

You can forget the description found in the New Testament which Matthew did not write at all which deals with the opening of the graves and the letting loose of the spirits supposedly contained therein who ran about in the streets of Jerusalem showing themselves to many (Matthew 27:52-53). This is strictly out of the imagination of the compilers of the Gospel and was written in many years later, and it is nothing more than a passage which the imaginative writer put into his work. Why people should want to believe in these representations of things that never happened is hard for me to understand. For in themselves they have no real significance except as a mere endeavor to make as dramatic and impressive as possible the supernatural circumstances they allege surrounded my death.

So you see I am not a savior because of my preferring the cross to my denying my messiahship and my Heavenly Father, but I was simply performing my mission to the end, and I would not be Jesus the Christ if I had not persisted to the end.

Atonement

I know that the belief in my sacrifice on the cross is the cornerstone of most of the churches, and that it is stated in the Bible and interpreted by the churches and the commentators on the Bible that my death carries with it a meaning of some price paid by me for the redemption of mankind from their sins (Matthew 20:28) and from the punishment that they would have to undergo for having committed these sins. It is said in various parts of the New Testament that my blood washes away all sin (Revelation 1:5), and that my death on the cross satisfies God's demands for justice; there are many similar expressions conveying the same idea. However, these sayings of the Bible were not written by the persons to whom they are ascribed, but by writers who, in their various translations and alleged reproductions of these writings, added to or eliminated from the original writings until the Bible became filled with false teachings and doctrines.

Christianity teaches that God sent his son, Jesus, to die on the cross to pay for the sins of the world. This assumes that the events leading up to my death and the men responsible were also necessary for this debt to be paid. If that be true, then why is it that Judas who betrayed me, Pilate who sentenced me and the Jews who clamored for my death are not considered to be saviours of humanity also even if you might say in a secondary sense only, instead of their being thought of as traitors and villains?

Nowhere in the Old Testament writings do we find as

an essential to God's promise of the Messiah that I had to die asphyxiated on a cross so that my Father in heaven, who had just revealed Himself in me as a God of Love, could satisfy a supposed sense of wrath for human sin. Some cults, mistaken in their understanding of the old Hebrew offerings, had made the loving Father the executioner of His own Son, a ritual which He had strikingly condemned in the case of Abraham. In accordance with this mistaken concept of the Hebrew offerings—a conception never advanced by me or the Apostles themselves, but by later pagan converts to Christianity—my blood in a similar manner as the pagan mystery cults believed is supposed in some mysterious way to immediately cleanse man's soul of all his evil thoughts, deeds and desires, doing vicariously that which man himself does not make the effort to do and which is supposed to make his soul fit to live with God.

The mistake, however, lies in the erroneous belief that the Hebrews thought there was efficacy in the shed blood of sacrificed animals. If they said that "life was in the blood" (Leviticus 17:11), it would be a scientific view devoid of any religious implications. The Hebrew system, as overwhelmingly demonstrated by the great prophets who brought the unchanging word of God to their people, uncompromisingly stresses forgiveness of sin through the turning to Jehovah and forsaking evil thoughts and ways. In this way only could sins be forgiven.

The offerings of animals in the Temple of Jerusalem were simply an outward act to show that man's heart was turned to God and that he was walking in the statutes of His Torah, of righteousness, justice and mercy. With the Babylonian captivity the Hebrews learned that man could walk in God's ways (Micah 6:8) without a Temple or sacrifices and that man's real offering to God, as expressed by Micah the prophet, consisted in the obeying of God's laws of justice, love and mercy.

Later, priestly insistence upon these rites and ceremonies were, for national purposes, only to keep the

Hebrews "pure" and "apart" from the Gentiles and the later pagan converts to Christianity. These converts were wedded to their own ritualistic cults and they adopted and blended the rites of the Hebrews with their own and converted the religion which I brought to become a religion of rite and ritual with salvation to be had through blood and sacrifice with me as the victim. In the reading of the passage in Luke and in Mark pertaining to the inheriting of eternal life, there is absolutely no reference to the vicarious atonement through my blood on the cross as the means of redemption (Luke 18:18-20).

When the rich young man appeared to me and asked me the question how he could obtain salvation for his soul (Matthew 19:16), the way the New Testament describes this meeting between us leads the reader to assume that my great message to mankind was nothing more than the Ten Commandments. In fact, several of the most important Commandments concerning man's love for God were omitted completely and mainly those dealing with man's relationship to other men were given. When the young man declared unto me that he had obeyed all of the Commandments and that he wished to know what else he had to buy or what else he had to do to merit salvation, I told him to give away all his property, become poor and to follow me (Matthew 19:21).

Well, this makes a very nice story in the New Testament and it is one which is usually read with interest and accepted by all those who understand that the Ten Commandments given to the children of Israel by Moses were in reality the laws of Jehovah pertaining to the moral code. However, they do not realize that if that was all that I had come to Palestine to teach, then there was no need of Jesus for Moses had already given these Commandments and I could do nothing more than to confirm what Moses had already proclaimed. It is a fact that I did teach the laws of Moses because they lead to purity, but not to the Divine Angelic state which cannot be reached through obedience to the moral code.

The conception of the vicarious atonement was a much later concept and never formed any part of the original writings of my disciples. This afterthought took form and shape when the teachings of the "New Heart" had been eliminated in favor of the conception of salvation to conciliate the old Jewish idea of sacrifice with the view of my being the sacrifice that would cleanse the sins of the world through the shedding of my blood. This conception of the atonement is all wrong for these writers were attempting to substitute me in place of the animals of sacrifice in the Jewish "plan of redemption". This is not justified by any teachings of mine nor by any of the true teachings of the disciples to whom I had explained the "plan of salvation" and what the atonement meant.

The consequence of this error is that the churches teach a salvation based on my sacrifice and death on the cross. This I deplore for it has no foundation in truth. No sacrifice made by me or anyone else can atone for the sins and misdeeds of another, not even if it be by the Messiah. God is the creator of life and of death, and my life was already a possession of God and, when I surrendered it, I did not give to God anything that was not already His. The absurdity of believing that God demanded that I should die in order to make a satisfactory payment is so apparent that I and all the spirits living in the kingdom of God wonder how mortals can believe such an unreasonable dogma.

The idea of a salvation based on the shedding of my blood has done much harm to retard the spiritual growth of believers in this doctrine while they live on earth and also when they go to the spirit world. I want the world to know that my mission was not to bring redemption through my suffering and death but to bring immortal life through God's Divine Love and mercy. Despite this great error there are enough truths in the Bible which have survived to lead men to salvation, especially those that show the way to attain moral perfection which was one of the objects of my teachings when on earth but not the great object of my mission.

REAPPEARANCE

Burial

My father, Joseph, came to Jerusalem with me on my last fatal mission which ended in my crucifixion. It was he who received permission from the authorities to take my body for burial after the Roman lancer, Coriginus, poked his lance into my side to determine my death (John 19:34).

When death came to me, my soul arose from the cross encased in its spirit body. I accompanied my dead body as it was carried by my followers to a place not far from the site of execution that my father had purchased for my burial. Nicodemus arrived with a mixture of myrrh and aloes and they cleansed my body and wound it in linen cloth with spices in the manner as was the custom of the day (John 19:39-41). I observed the events waiting until the ritual of burial had been accomplished, then I ascended to the spirit world from the Mount of Olives. My entrance was a glorious one, I was welcomed by many spirits and the Father. I proclaimed to the inhabitants the rebestowal of the availability of Divine Love and the possibility of at-onement with God through receiving It.

The next day the chief priests came to Pilate and appealed to him that the sepulcher be made secure until the third day so that I would not arise as promised. Pilate agreed and sent guards to seal the tomb and set a watch (Matthew 27:65-66). My father was very interested in the precautions taken to prove that I would not arise from the tomb, so he kept watch along with the soldiers. Because he feared the Jews as well as the Romans, he sought to conceal his identity from them by taking the name Joseph of Arimathea which in Hebrew means "father of the prophet".

On the third day I left the spirit realms and returned to the earth plane and I entered the tomb in my spirit body. I dematerialized my battered body of flesh and blood into the surrounding atmosphere. I understood and had the power to call into operation certain laws of nature which enabled me to do this. I then materialized a new body with the elements drawn from the universe which to a degree seemed like flesh and blood and which closely resembled my own body. I was able to accomplish this by the spiritual culling of eternal cosmic elements from the universe to give an appearance of flesh which conforms to a process of the building of organic molecules around a spirit body. This rebuilding, or materialization, took place in a way similar to that in which ectoplasm borrowed from mediums is used to enable a spirit body to be visible to mortal eyes. This process of transformation from cosmic matter to substance like unto flesh without benefit of a bodily organism took place by spiritual energy being applied with my own Divine energy.

I unwrapped the linen cloth which had covered my body and folded it neatly and placed it in a corner of the tomb (John 20:6). At the time I did not realize that it would be the means of a fairly good representation of the appearance of my countenance. I left the tomb by passing through the rock which barred the entrance. The stone blocking the entrance to the cave was later rolled away by the bright spirit in the form of a young man who was sent by God for this purpose (Matthew 28:2). The strength he displayed in this task was obtained through the transmission of energy conveyed to him by the many spirits who were present at the time. He used a guard whom he put into a trance by suggestion as the means by which he obtained the necessary ectoplasm to bring about his materialization.

When the guards realized my body had disappeared, they relayed what they had seen to the chief priests who, after consultation, decided they would bribe the guards to say to the people that my body had been stolen from the tomb by my disciples. The guards were promised by the chief priests to be kept in good standing with Pilate if he should hear of the deception (Matthew 28:12-14). My father was there when the angel came and rolled the stone away. He was frightened and overcome when he saw the shining one standing guard at the tomb entrance. He heard Mary Magdalene inquiring as to the whereabouts of her beloved Master (John 20:2).

When I revealed myself to Mary, she did not recognize me for my appearance was not the same as that of the Jesus whose body had been entombed. Although I did have the same countenance and eyes and voice of affection that were familiar to her, my physical appearance was different and she thought that I was the gardener (John 20:15). Peter arrived and was astonished. He did not comprehend the events and was bewildered (Luke 24:12) as were the others notwithstanding what I had told him prior to the crucifixion.

No one at the time understood the power I had over matter. People have taught and believed that my body arose from the tomb and that the bodies of mortals will also arise at the time of the Great Resurrection. This is not the case because the body which dies disintegrates into its elements and never again will these elements form that same body. There are laws set forth by the Creator which are familiar to mortals from their observations of the workings of nature that prove the impossibility of such an occurrence.

After my death my father was confused as to my mission, bewildered at the turn of events and he feared for his personal safety. He was also terribly disappointed at my being "King of the Jews" in the sign of the cross only, in which they inscribed me as such in several languages (Luke 23:38).

Resurrection

Prior to my death I never said there would be a

resurrection of my physical body, for the body that is once laid in the grave will never be resurrected. What I did tell my followers was that I would not die because my soul was immortal and therefore not subject to death. However, I had great difficulty being understood because of the lack of spirituality of the Jews at the time and their inability to perceive that I was not talking of physical death but of spiritual death.

The body of flesh is of matter and like all matter is used for life on the earth only and can never be used for any function or for clothing any spirit in the spirit world. I know that it has been written that certain of the prophets of old were translated into the spirit heavens clothed in their fleshly bodies (2 Kings 2:11), but this is not true for it is impossible that such a thing can be. The same laws apply to the physical body of the saint as to that of the sinner; flesh and blood cannot inherit the kingdom and no belief or teaching can make that true which is not true.

When I said "he that liveth and believeth on me shall never die" (John 11:25), what I meant was that the man whose soul was not dead in sin but believed in the truths which I declared, that God is waiting with His Love to fill his soul with Its Essence, and that that man, who by his faith received this Love would never die.

My teachings were that the mortal would arise in his spirit body at death, not in a new body made specially for this occasion, but one that had been with that mortal throughout his earthly life. This spirit body (1 Corinthians 15:44) is necessary to a soul's existence and is that part which contains the senses and is the seat of the reasoning powers. The resurrection of the body that I taught is the resurrection of the spirit body, not from death for it never dies, but rather from its envelopment in the material form. Thus, you can realize that the resurrection will not take place at some unknown day in the future but at the very moment when the physical body dies. This resurrection applies to all mortals for all who have ever lived and died have been resurrected, and all hereafter who shall live and die will also be resurrected. So you see the belief that the spirits of men who have died the natural death are resting in their graves or in oblivion, in order to come again to life and be resurrected (1 Thessalonians 4:16), is not true.

When I said, "I am the way, the truth, and the life" (John 14:6), I did not mean, "wait until I die and then I will demonstrate the resurrection", or "when you see me ascend to heaven, then I will become the resurrection and you will know it." The meaning of this saying and my mission was that I had come to show the way to become a partaker of God's gift of Divine Love. This Love was first made available to the first man and the first woman (the First Parents) who were created just a little lower than angels (Psalms 8:5). They were given the privilege to become Divine Angels and to acquire Divine and immortal souls through prayer to God. Instead, they chose to be independent of God and thought they could become Divine and immortal through their own efforts. Of course the parts played by the apple and the snake and the devil are not literally true, but they are merely symbolic of the elements that entered into their temptation and fall.

With their disobedience, or refusal to seek Divine Love in the way prescribed by God, they lost the privilege of receiving It for themselves and their descendants. With the loss of this privilege man was limited to make his way in the material world mainly through those finite human qualities, namely the will, the intellect and moral fiber. The gift of this potentiality was not in itself the actual bestowal upon humanity of the Divine qualities of God; such potentiality merely made it possible for humans to acquire those qualities by aspiration and effort. In fact, before the bestowal no one could obtain the condition and qualities which this potentiality made possible by any aspirations or efforts on their part no matter how great the effort might be for these qualities were simply not available. This possibility had not been restored to humanity in all the long centuries and humans had remained in this condition of death until it was brought to light by me.

So you see the resurrection from the dead that I taught arises from the fact that God had withdrawn the potential of receiving His Divine Love from the First Parents and that with my coming God had rebestowed upon all humanity the privilege to seek for and to receive His Divine Love which would make them at-one with Him and immortal. Now in order to obtain this resurrection, one must seek for and find the Divine Love and thereby become a child of the true resurrection. This was not possible for any prophet, seer, reformer or teacher of any faith before my coming no matter how excellent their moral teachings and private lives might have been.

When I received God's precious gift of Divine Love into my soul and acquired possession of God's Divine Nature, I realized my at-onement with God and the consciousness of my immortality and I knew that I had been lifted up unto everlasting life.

Road to Emmaus

It became impossible for my father to remain in Palestine having been pointed out as the father of the crucified Jesus. He was afraid of the consequences, both political as well as religious, of my crucifixion. That afternoon my father, under the concealed name of Cleopas, and my brother Thomas, hastened to Emmaus (Luke 24:13) to escape what they thought was going to be certain arrest and crucifixion as had happened to me. I went after them in my new body in order to bring them back to Jerusalem so that all my disciples would be together when they saw me.

Thomas had begun to doubt and his attitude could have been disastrous to the entire "plan of salvation" by bringing pessimism and skepticism into the minds of my followers. That is why I went to Emmaus and had Thomas and Cleopas recognize me when I broke bread with them (Luke 24:30-31). At that time the Divine Love flowed into their souls, and they immediately regained their faith and returned with me to Jerusalem to face whatever dangers there might be. So on the next Friday Thomas was there and poked his fingers into my side which gave him faith (John 20:27) and this crucial time was overcome in victory.

In Jerusalem where all my disciples were assembled, I told them that all the power of heaven and earth comes to those who partake of the Divine Love of God (Matthew 28:18). I said to them, "go, therefore, and teach the way to receive this Love and every man can be baptized by the Holy Spirit through his desire; by this the "Christ" will develop in your soul and will be with you all the days of your life, forever with me and at-one with God" (Matthew 28:20).

My return was necessary in order to show my disciples that I was still alive even after death by crucifixion. For at this time in their spiritual development this phenomenon was the proof in their eyes that I was the Messiah. Their real understanding of my messiahship came to them at the Pentecost when the Divine Love was conveyed into their souls with such power and abundance that they knew I had come to bring the very Essence of God to humanity.

My death was a great personal tragedy in the lives of my closest and dearest. My mother stayed with John and his family until her death (John 19:27). His love and affection for her were a great source of consolation. In the loss of my life not merely physically but also in the ties of my family, I gained life in the spirit world where every member of my family is present and often with me. They now fully realize my mission as the Messiah and know of my love for them.

Pentecost

My disciples and followers who had remained faithful to me after my crucifixion had the realization that my mission was a spiritual one. They were very much affected by the brutal manner in which my death had been imposed upon me. Their sorrow was deep and continual, and it was their love for me and grieving that turned their hearts and souls towards God in a great yearning of love and aspiration. They loved me wholeheartedly as their rabbi and they were filled with a deep grief and love that made their souls ready to receive the Divine Love when it was poured out upon them.

It culminated in a great abundance conveyed to them fifty days after my death at the time of the pentecostal showering upon their souls of God's precious Essence. It came into their souls with a great inflowing and burning of the heart and with the sound of a mighty rushing wind which shook the room where they were assembled and filled them with its power (Acts 2:2). This meant that the Divine Love came into their souls in such abundance that they were shaken to the extent that they thought the building in which they were assembled was disturbed. But, in this, they were mistaken for the presence of the Holy Spirit does not affect things of inanimate nature but is confined to and is exclusively for the souls of God's children. The Divine Love implanted into their souls by the Holy Spirit did not come all at once but had been building up within their souls for those fifty days.

After the Pentecost my disciples had a clearer understanding of my mission. The inflowing of Divine Love absorbed their human or natural love and gave them the faith and courage to set out into the world to preach the true doctrines of my mission on earth—the Love of the Father for His children and the fact that this Love was waiting for any and all who should seek It.

The Pentecost marked the end of the Jewish dispensation or the end of the Jewish world. For at this time the Divine Love, which was first bestowed upon me, was now being granted to my followers in abundance. The Mosaic laws, the highest available to mankind prior to my coming, were superceded by the New Covenant (Hebrews 8:8) of the Heart and the "rebirth" of the soul in God's Love.

The Holy Spirit

The churches of today believe and teach that the Holy Spirit is the third part of the Trinity which has attached to it various names such as the Spirit of God, Spirit of the Lord, Spirit of Christ, Spirit of Truth, Spirit of Glory, the Paraclete, the Advocate, the Comforter or Strengthener.

The Holy Spirit is as invisible as the wind yet it is just as real and existing. It is that part of God that manifests His Love, care and presence to His children. The Holy Spirit does not communicate with mortals or spirits directly nor does it appeal to their reasoning faculties. It cannot instruct or inform but operates upon the human mind indirectly to influence the reasoning faculties. I have never been instructed by the Holy Spirit whose function is not that of teaching, but that of conveying God's Divine qualities to His children.

The spirit of God which is not the Holy Spirit, though equally a part of God, demonstrates to humans the operation of God in other directions and for other purposes. This spirit is God's creative spirit, caring spirit and the spirit that makes effective His laws and designs for the governing of the universe. This spirit has been manifest throughout all eternity and is the spirit which has been described in Genesis; hovering over the face of the earth (Genesis 1:2), working on and developing it in preparation of the day when life and living beings could exist and survive on it.

All things have their existence and operation and growth in the spirit of God and only in this spirit which is evidenced in many and varied ways in human experience.

Hence, when people say that they live and move and have their being in God, this means that they live and move and have their being in the spirit of God. This spirit is the source of life and light and health and numerous other blessings that humans possess and enjoy. It is omnipresent, universal in its existence and workings.

The Holy Spirit is as distinctive as the human soul is distinctive from all other creations. The Holy Spirit is that part of God which has to do exclusively with the relationship between God's Soul and His children's souls. The subject of its operation is the Divine Love and the object of its workings is the human soul. The great goal to be reached by its operation is the transforming of the human soul from the image of the Divine as it was created into the very Essence and Substance of the Divine, with immortality as the result.

This gift is so high and sacred and merciful that the part of God which carries His Divine Love to his children and accomplishes the great miracle of "rebirth" is called The Holy Spirit.

Trinity

I know that orthodox Christians generally believe and classify the Holy Spirit as a part of the Godhead being identical and equal to God the Father though having a distinct and different personality. The orthodox preachers and theological writers teach that it is a fact that the Father, the Son and the Holy Ghost are one, co-equal and co-existing, and this fact is the "great mystery" of God. Men have been told that they should not endeavor to fathom this mystery because the sacred things of God are His own and the churches teach that it is unlawful for men to enter into these secrets.

Well, this declaration and admonition is very wise as the wisdom of men goes and saves the expounders of these doctrines of mystery from having to attempt to explain what they cannot explain because it is impossible for them to unravel that which, as a fact, has no existence. All through the ages men have sought to understand this "great mystery", as they call it, and have been unsuccessful. The early Church fathers met with the same defeat in their endeavors to understand this mystery and then, because of such defeat, declared the explanation of this doctrine to be a secret of God and not to be inquired into by man for it belonged to God alone. Thus, from the beginning of the established Church after my death and the death of my Apostles, it was declared that this doctrine of the trinity, one in three and three in one, was the vital foundation stone of their visible Church's existence.

Now, from time to time there arose men who had more enlightenment than their brothers in the Church, and they attempted to gainsay the truth of this doctrine and declared and maintained that there was only one God, the God of Abraham. But they were in the minority and, because they did not act with the more powerful, their views were rejected. Thus, this "great mystery" became the Church's sacred symbol of truth, unexplainable and therefore more certain and entitled to even more credence. It seems to be the tendency of men's minds, or at least of those who believe in the Bible as the inspired word of God, to welcome and encourage as the more wonderful and important and the more to be cherished, those things which savor of the mysterious rather than those things which may be read and understood.

It is true that I discussed Abraham with the Jews and how he would have welcomed my appearance in Jerusalem, but I never saw Abraham until I passed over into the spirit world regardless what the Gospels declare I said. Nor did I say that before Abraham was, I am (John 8:58), which would make me the second part of a supposed trinity and a part of the Godhead. This is an insertion which was put into John's Gospel a hundred years or more after John had written his original work.

I never claimed to be part of the "Godhead" for

nowhere in the Bible is there any saying of mine that God is tripartite consisting of the Father, the Son and the Holy Ghost. And, as a matter of fact, never when I was on earth, did I teach such a doctrine, but only this: that the Father is God and the only God, and that I, Jesus, am his Son and the first fruits of the resurrection (1 Corinthians 15:23), and that the Holy Ghost is God's messenger for conveying the Divine Love and, as such, brings the Comforter (John 14:26).

Evangelization

When I sent my disciples forth in pairs to teach (Mark 6:7), I did not enable them to heal the sick or cure the blind, the lame and the crippled because it was not in my power to do so. Such power could only be obtained from God as a result of the Divine Love being in their souls to such an extent that they would be possessed of the power to cure (Luke 9:1). This power could then be used in obedience to the prayers for healing on the part of the disciples. So the New Testament is wrong in that particular for they could not heal until the day of the Pentecost when the Divine Love flowed into their souls in such abundance that they were given the power.

After seeing my newly materialized body at the tomb, my father experienced a great breakdown in his beliefs about my mission and he began to see it in its spiritual sense. When his confusion and bitter disappointment subsided, he gained faith in my mission as the Messiah, and to calm his anguished heart he evangelized with some of my disciples on several of the islands off the coast of Greece, notably Patmos and Cyprus. After many years he made his way to Great Britain but he died there soon after. The supernatural event connected with the flowering of a branch has no factual relation to the events which mark his stay in that island empire.

My brother Thomas was one of my Apostles, my brother Jacob founded the Jerusalem sect and my brother

Juda became a disciple. These followers and others had managed to plant into the souls of succeeding decades of people the seeds of prayer to the Father for Divine Love which transforms the soul and gives eternal life.

Peter

There is nothing in the Gospels that indicates Peter should have received primacy for, as a matter of fact, he was not the first to recognize that I was the Messiah the first to do so was John, the Baptist. When the Gospels were written, the Christian movement was under way and the account (Matthew 16:16), which stressed that Peter acknowledged me to be the Christ does not show that I had ever bestowed leadership upon him, and any statements which indicate that Peter discovered my identity through heavenly Grace are not true. This was simply inserted to strengthen and give authority to the Church's claim that I had bestowed primacy upon him as my successor.

I never gave Peter the keys to the kingdom for the only key is the Divine Love which can be possessed by all mortals and spirits who desire the key to open the gates. Nor did I give Peter the power to bind and loosen in heaven those things which he might find it appropriate for him to do on earth (Matthew 16:19) for this was something which I never said and never gave. This came from a later Greek writer and was written into the Gospel of Matthew as legal authority. I could not make Peter a representative of God on earth nor ratify those acts which he felt should be done for only God Himself could designate a mortal to be His representative on earth as had been done in the case of the Hebrew prophets and John, the Baptist, and, in a different way, myself.

Now with respect to the saying, "Upon this rock I shall build my church" (Matthew 16:18), this is a distortion in my sayings to Peter made by the later Gospel writers. So when I said, "Thou art Peter," I did not say upon this rock

I shall build my church meaning neither upon Peter nor myself, but upon the "Rock of Ages"—the Father through the Divine Love that had been brought to light with my coming.

Peter's leadership was recognized because he was the eldest and held the respect of the other disciples and was looked up to because of his close relationship with me. Oftentimes I had addressed him while I was teaching my disciples and had favored him by taking him with me to the Mount of Transfiguration. Peter spoke boldly at Pentecost and he preached and healed on the Mediterranean coast and in various parts of the Greek world. He never recalled from the dead the person of Tabitha or Dorcas in Joppa, as recorded in the New Testament (Acts 9:40), but healed her of her illness. No one can recall to life a person who has truly died.

Peter continued my work and gained in love and conviction of the truth. His preeminence was the result of the practical turn of affairs for at that time he took the leadership upon himself which was enhanced when he sent Barnabas to Asia Minor on various missions. Peter worked consistently to establish the Church and eliminate undesirable traits to make it a firm religious institution. He decided that many innovations had to be adopted if the pagans were to become believers in me as the Messiah.

Peter made his way to Rome where he was arrested but then released from prison, not by any miracle of angels coming to take the irons from his wrists and to open the door (Acts 12:7), but because some of his jailers became believers in my teachings and mission and were converted. They had seen Peter heal and preferred the things of the spirit than to see him languish in prison and perhaps to suffer the same fate as I.

After my death questions concerning the movement

were referred to Peter for solution. He showed himself
capable of holding the leadership and also because Rome
was the leader of the known world at the time and, as
Peter was the authority of the greatest church in the
greatest city of the world, he became the authority over
the entire Christian world. He lived in Rome for nearly
fifteen years and was crucified there about the same time
as was Paul, shortly before the destruction of the Temple
at Jerusalem.

Paul

Paul was a very learned man among the Jews and was
a strict believer and follower of the Pharisees' doctrines.
He knew nothing about the Divine Love for he had never
experienced it nor did he know what it was intellectually.
My summons to him was not only for the purpose of
stopping the persecution of my people (Acts 9:4), but also
for the further purpose to enlist him in my cause because
my followers were not educated or learned men. I
realized that my doctrines and truths must be preached
among not only the learned Jews but also among the
gentile philosophers. I saw that I must have a disciple
who would have the mental qualifications to present my
truths to these learned men in a convincing way, and be
able to withstand the logic and reasoning of these gentile
philosophers.

When I spoke to Paul on his way to Damascus, he was
felled to the ground by the brightness of the great light
that shone about him (Acts 9:3). Paul heard what I said
and answered me and went into the town, but he was not
blind nor did the prophet Ananias do anything to him in
the way of curing any physical blindness (Acts 9:17). He
only helped to open the spiritual blindness of Paul and
showed him the way to the Father's Love and the
kingdom.

Paul did not have the love that John did. Whenever
John would come in close communion with the common

71

people, he could by the great power and influence of his love persuade them to embrace and receive my truths and, as a consequence, feel the inflowing of the Holy Spirit. Paul did not have this love to that degree to be enabled by virtue of its power or influence to convince and compel his hearers to receive my truths and embrace that faith in my teachings which would cause them to seek the Love of God. Hence, his mission was more intended to be the teaching of my truths to the intellect and mental perceptions of a large number of people of greater intellectual development than those with whom John and the other disciples would come in contact.

Paul eventually acquired Divine Love to a considerable degree but not sufficiently to prevent him at times in his early ministry from doubting my calling him to do this work. This doubt was the besetting sin or thorn in the flesh (2 Corinthians 12:7) from which he suffered. Nevertheless, he became a wonderful power to spread my truths and to convince men that the Love of the Father was the one great possession to be obtained. He further caused them to believe in me as the "Son of God" and His messenger to declare to the world the great plan of man's redemption. When he said, "they see through a glass darkly," but then they shall see face to face, and when they do, they will see such evidences (1 Corinthians 13:12) and manifestations of the Father's Love that they will know that they and their sinning brothers are all sons of the Father.

Paul never taught that I was God nor did he believe that I was, and whenever it is set forth that he did say that, or rather what the Bible says on that subject (Hebrews 1:8) is interpreted to mean that I am God, that interpretation is erroneous. You may also rest assured that Hebrews was not written by Paul who had already entered the spirit world many years before this epistle had been written. Instead, it was written by a Greek supporter of the Hellenistic turn Christianity had taken after Titus' destruction of Jerusalem in 70 A.D.

Authenticity of the Bible

The churches differ in their creeds and government and interpretations of the Bible yet they, the orthodox churches, are all founded on the Bible. They cannot teach greater or other truths than the Bible contains. Hence, if man is seeking for truths that are not contained in the Bible, his inquiries cannot be answered by those whose knowledge is confined strictly to the teachings of the Bible. While the Bible even as now written is a grand old book and does preserve a number of my teachings, it is not the true mouthpiece of God in very many particulars and is a stumbling block to man's acquiring a correct knowledge of the truths of God. I must tell you that God's truths can be understood by all men and without the need of a highly developed intellect, and that any religion which requires the exercise of the mental faculties to a greater extent than what is required in the ordinary affairs of life cannot be a true religion.

My disciples and followers did not commence to place in the form of a manuscript my teachings or the experience of my life until a long time after I had left the earth. They expected my speedy return at which time I was to become their king and legislator. Hence, they saw no occasion or necessity to preserve in the form of writings the truths in which I had instructed them.

The Bible, was compiled from many writings and compilers in those early times, differed in their opinions just as men do now regarding religious truth. The more powerful of these men had authority to declare what should be accepted according to their interpretations of the manuscripts that were being copied. These men put forth the copies to be made in accordance with their ideas and, I may say, desires to attain wealth, power and control over the common people in their beliefs and observances of worship. They, in turn, put forth such productions to be true copies of the originals. As these copies were successively made, the preceding ones were destroyed.

Hence, the earliest existing writings of the Gospels came from copies which came into existence many years after the original manuscripts from which they are claimed to have been compiled were written.

These men over time had become less spiritual than my disciples, hence their thoughts and efforts became more centered in building up the Church than in attempting to develop and preserve my great spiritual teachings. The God of Love then, to a large extent, became a God of hatred and wrath who inflicted punishment upon those who dared to disobey those injunctions that the hierarchy of the Church placed upon the common people as being the demands and will of God.

When the Emperor Constantine adopted Christianity as the state religion of Rome in 312 A.D., it was not because he was a believer in the Christian teachings but it was for political purposes. His desire was to destroy the powers of his antagonists who were believers in and the worshippers of the gods of paganism. Constantine made

Christianity the state religion to obtain power and the allegiance of the majority of the people of the empire. The Christians were very numerous and were people of such intense convictions that not even the threat of death could remove or change their convictions. Constantine knew that once he had gained their allegiance, he would have a following that could not be overthrown by those who were worshippers of the old gods.

During his time in office as emperor Constantine never accepted the teachings of the Christians as a revelation of truth. He did not establish the canonicity of the Bible or determine and legalize the doctrines which were declared and made binding by the conventions of the leaders of the Church. Constantine did, however, give his sanction and official approval, but the doctrines were not established by him because he never became a Christian nor understood its teachings, notwithstanding all the fantastical and miraculous things which have been written about his conversion to Christianity.

THE SECOND COMING

Prince Michael

I know that it is expected that I will return as Prince Michael to establish a kingdom on earth and take unto me those whose names are written in the book and destroy those whose names are not therein written (Revelation 20:12-15). This, however, is not the case, because when I brought to light that my Heavenly Father had bestowed upon humanity the great possibility to obtain His Divine Love, never thereafter arose the necessity for the existence or coming of another Christ.

Some Christians also believe that at this time they will be of the elect and become princes and sub-rulers of the kingdom. No, this will never be for I have already come and am now in the world working to turn men's hearts to the Father and to teach them the way by which all men may become at-one with God by their receiving His Divine Love into their hearts.

I never taught my disciples or hearers that my reign would be an earthly one or that I was to be "King of the Jews" in any other than a spiritual sense. For men will not need me as a visible king with the powers and armies of the spirit world in visible form to subdue the evil that exists. There is no Satan to fight against me or my followers and the fact is that I am already fighting for the redemption of men's souls. The only devils or evil spirits who are trying to influence mortals to evil thoughts and actions are the spirits of men who once lived on earth and who still retain all their sins, wickedness and the evil that exists in their hearts.

The concept that I am the Judge of the world and that I will come one day to judge it is an entirely false and illusionary one and was never taught by me. I do not have the power to judge, as the New Testament claims, and this passage "For the Father judgeth no man, but hath commanded all judgement to the Son" (John 5:22), must be interpreted that the Father indeed does not sentence but that man sentences himself through the memories of his misdeeds in which the law of compensation acts upon these inharmonies to purge him through a process of purification.

There will be no battle of Armageddon except only as each man or the soul of each man is now fighting the battle between sin and righteousness. This is the only battle that will ever be fought between the Prince of Peace and the so-called Satan for each soul must fight its own battle and in that fight the powers of God, by His instruments, will be used to help overcome the great enemy sin. So you see, it does much harm to those who believe that I, as the Prince of Peace, will come in mighty power and in one fell swoop destroy evil and all who personify it and thereby do the work which each individual must do through his own efforts.

Religion of the Future

There will be a religion of the future, a comprehensive and final one, and it will be founded upon the teachings which I am now sending to the earth. These teachings will fulfill all the promises of the Scriptures of my "Second Coming." In no other way will I ever come to mortals of the earth. These teachings will only add to the old beliefs that all humanity can embrace and follow but will also lead those who follow them to complete happiness. This religion will be inclusive of all the other religions, so far as the truths which they contain are concerned, with the addition of the greatest of all truths affecting mortals—the "New Heart" and the transformation of the human soul into the Divine.

I know that many things are believed because they are ancient or bear the authority of the sages of olden days, their forefathers or some great saint or philosopher who lived many centuries ago. Such a basis for accepting something as true, although worthy of consideration and examination, does not of itself afford any certainty of the truth. Real truths, whether from ancient times or of the present, are the same truths for truths never change or assume new forms no matter what the condition of mortals in their intellectual or spiritual development. Truths are being revealed today and are constantly being revealed as time goes on and they should be accepted with as much credence and satisfaction as truths that were disclosed in ancient times.

The minds of mortals were given to them to exercise by query, investigation and search. Never was it contemplated in human creation that the time would come when man should accept anything as the ultimate truth and cease making inquiries. Truths are so many, so great and so deep that humanity has acquired only a smattering of them. To rest now, at this point, in the belief that there is nothing more to be learned in the way of truth would violate and subvert the very object of human creation.

The churches declare and try to enforce the declaration that it is not possible to discover essential principles of spiritual truth to any further extent than is set forth in the religious Scriptures. Therefore, they claim it is contrary to God's will that man should seek further for additional truths. Instead, they should accept without question the sayings of the particular dogmas or creeds of the churches. This has been the demand of the churches and their members have, by and large, acquiesced without question or doubt. This acquiescence is one of the major reasons why humanity has not progressed further not only in its spiritual nature but also in what may be called its human love qualities. People have remained satisfied and content to cling to the idea that what was believed centuries ago is the only truth of today.

One of the most damnable doctrines taught by the churches is that of the unpardonable sin. This false doctrine will have no place in the religion of the future for this doctrine for this is a thing that has no existence either in the world of mortals or in the world of spirits. Every soul has the opportunity for redemption and God loves those who believe in Him just as He loves those who do not believe in Him, the only difference is that the believers may partake of His Divine Essence.

Great Millennium

As it is commonly understood the Great Millennium is a time or period of a thousand years when peace will reign on the earth and the devil, as is said, will be bound and not permitted to roam to cause sin, destruction of souls, sickness and the other problems that now so generally beset mortals (Revelation 20:2).

Sin was never created by God nor is it a product or emanation of God, but is wholly the result of the wrongful exercise of man's appetites and will. Humans have a double set of emotions, one on the basic animal level and the other for the higher living, development and fulfillment of the spiritual values. Sin occurs when man's material desires are permitted to overcome the desires of his spiritual nature. With sin comes all the evils, discords and disharmonies that constitute man's manner of living his earthly life. Until these things which are not a part of his original nature but which are the creation of the perversion of that nature are eliminated from his thoughts, desires and appetites, the Millennium will never be established.

As a preliminary to the ushering in of this time of peace and purity, man must cease to believe that it will appear with my coming in a manifested physical way as a mortal conqueror who might come with legions of followers (Jude 14), the noise of drums, the force of arms and greatness of power to subdue my enemies. This will never be for no man is my enemy but all are my brothers, and I am not making and never will make war on any human being but only on the sin and defilement that is within his soul. This war can never be waged by power or force of legions of angels for so great is the power of God's gift of man's free will and so respected is its freedom of action by the Father, that there is no power in heaven or earth that can or will change a sinful soul into a pure one by force, threats or conquering legions of angels even though they might be led by me which will not happen.

The soul is the real person, and that soul can be made pure and sinless only when that soul desires and consents that such a condition may become its own. It should not be difficult to understand how the erroneous belief that I will come in the semblance of a mortal conqueror and establish this great time of peace is doing much harm and delaying the actual time of the coming of this greatly desired period. The result of this belief upon men is they think that everything is to be accomplished by my work and nothing by themselves except to believe in my coming and wait and be ready to be snatched up to the clouds (1 Thessalonians 4:17). Men also claim that I, by my great power and the fact that they believe that I will come again to earth and establish a kingdom, will in the twinkling of an eye make them fit subjects (1 Corinthians 15:52).

No, this can never be the way in which the Great Millennium will be established and the sooner men discard this belief and seek the true way to purity and perfection the sooner the hope and expectations of this greatly desired period will be realized.

End of the World

No one, whether in the flesh or in spirit, has the omniscience of God nor the vision to foretell what will happen centuries ahead, this power belongs only to God.

Thus all the attempted applications of prophecies contained in the Bible of future happenings are futile and without justification.

I know it is expected by most Christians that the world will someday come to an end (Mark 13:31). The world, meaning the earth, will not have an end in the sense of annihilation but will continue to revolve on its axis, have seed time and harvest, produce and reproduce those things which are necessary to sustain life. It will continue to have its appropriate seasons of heat and cold and move along in its orbit as it now does until some change of which I do not know may come and destroy it.

Humans will continue to be born, live a short time and die a physical death; for each individual, the end of the material world comes at death and thereafter habitation will be in the spirit world. If all mortals at some time will have to die a physical death, then why should it be necessary for God to include in His "plan of salvation" the destruction of the material world? For planets and worlds and stars to crash together and be destroyed would mean that the orderly workings of God's laws must be interfered with in order that men might be saved or destroyed.

This will never be; however, there shall come a time of wars and rumors of war and times of trouble such as has never been, and then shall come the end (Matthew 24:6). Not the wars of cannons' roars or the bursting of shells or the mutilating of flesh or the making of widows and orphans or the ruthless changing of mortals into spirits, but the wars of the spirits of good and evil, of love and hate, of purity and sin, of joy and despair and of knowledge of truth and belief in error—all to be fought in the souls of men with such intensity and earnestness to create such mind and spirit trouble as has never been.

Then shall come the end of the world, the world of evil and sin and despair and hatred and belief in error. This is the world that shall pass away, and then the world of truth and love and peace and goodwill shall be established on earth forever. The earth will become so peaceful and filled with such love and kindness that it will seem as if the City of God has been lowered down from heaven onto it.

Kingdom of Heaven

As I said when I was on earth, "narrow is the gate and narrow is the way which leads to life eternal and few there be who enter therein" (Matthew 7:14). Now this saying applies to the spiritual world as well as to the material world. So let me urge upon all to seek the straight and narrow way for only by it can humans come to the full enjoyment of what the Father has provided for them. I cannot tell you of all the wonders that He has prepared for His children who enter His kingdom because there are no words that will properly convey my meaning. However, it was truly said, "that no eye has seen nor mind conceived the wonderful things that await the true child of God" (1 Corinthians 2:9).

I must tell you that the kingdom of heaven is a place as well as a condition. There is nothing nebulous or impalpable about the kingdom nor is it a reflection or image of the soul's condition, but everything in it is real and substantial and lasting and not subject to decay or deterioration of any kind. The many mansions of which I spoke exist in my Father's house (John 14:2) and are real and permanent and not dependent upon the condition of the soul for their existence. However, the condition of the soul does determine just where it shall occupy and find its harmony and happiness. The Father has provided that the soul shall have a place corresponding to its condition where it will live and from where it may progress. When the soul finds a habitation, it is a place already prepared for that soul (John 14:3) in accord with its true condition.

Heaven as a place is real and independent of the state of the soul; otherwise, it would be a place of confusion and of appearances and disappearances without stability or abiding qualities. The mansions are there and whether or not they shall have occupants depends on the harmony of souls with God's laws. They are made of the most beautiful materials, a substance that you might think of as white alabaster and furnished with everything that is suited to make the inhabitants content. Above all is the wonderful quality of Love which is always present and fills their souls to overflowing and keeps them in one continuous state of peace and joy and happiness.

Now regarding the words; "It is easier for a camel to pass through the eye of a needle than for a rich man to enter the kingdom of heaven" (Matthew 19:24). I did not use the word camel at all for it has no association with a needle, and it never occurred to me to use that word as found in many versions of the New Testament. What I did say was, "It is easier for a rope to pass through the eye of a needle than for a rich man to enter the kingdom of heaven". This would suggest that the rich man who is attached to his earthly treasures would be less interested in the things of the spiritual. Therefore, it is conceivable that the poor man could enter the kingdom more readily than the rich man.

The parable evoked the question from Peter, "Who then can be saved?" (Matthew 19:25). I answered that through individual effort and earnest prayer to God for Divine Love all souls can be saved as well as transformed whereby all sin and desire to sin are eradicated from that soul and, in this way, that soul may enter the kingdom of heaven. This sermon was eliminated by later copyists and revisionists and in its stead they wrote; "With men this is impossible, but with God all things are possible." (Matthew 19:26)

So attractive is the accumulation of wealth and the gaining of fame or position that when once successful, man naturally devotes his whole waking time and thoughts to these efforts. As a consequence very little of his short time on earth is given to thoughts of the higher kind or of the cultivation of his spiritual qualities. The sin is that of omission, and it is a sure one in its results because the thoughts and efforts used to accomplish material results do not help the soul's development of the spiritual side of man's nature. When man comes to lay his burdens down and pass into the land of spirits, he will find that he is poor indeed for the eternal part of his being has little development and his soul is fitted only for the place where those who have laid up their riches on earth can go. So you see entry into the kingdom is an individual matter and depends not upon a man's worldly possessions or lack of them, but upon his soul's condition and desire. So I say what good is it for a man to gain the world if he is to lose his soul (Matthew 16:26).

God's kingdom is not a finished one for it is still in the process of formation and is open to the entry of all spirits who seek it in the way provided. No one will be excluded who, with all the longings of his soul, aspires to pass through its gates. There will however come a time when the kingdom will be a finished one and then it will become the only place of my love and labor. When I said, "work while it is day, for the night cometh when no man can work" (John 9:4), I meant that while the kingdom is open, work must continue to build it with the souls of humans transformed into Divine Angels. When its doors shall close, the work of the angelic laborers will cease on the earth, for they will no longer be needed because the earth shall be restored to the paradise that it once had been.

THE TEACHINGS

First Man and First Woman

God created the world and, when I say the "world", I mean both the physical and the spiritual worlds. These creations were merely changes in form or composition of what had already existed and will exist forever as elements of the universe. The earth on which you live did not always have an existence as a planet and neither did the firmament, the great galaxy of planets and stars, but they were not created from nothing nor was there chaos. In God's economy of being there is never any chaos, if there were, it would be caused by the absence or failure of God's own laws of harmony and that does not happen.

The first man and the first woman were not made of the dust of the ground but were made of the elements that existed in the universe of a different order than the mere dust of the ground (Genesis 2:7) and were so created by God for the purpose of forming their physical bodies. They were made at the same time and not one out of the rib of the other (Genesis 2:22). Therefore, the man and the woman are equal in their dignity and in the relationship which they bear to God, and one is of just as much importance in the sight of God as is the other.

The man was created stronger physically than the woman, and he was also given a stronger mentality for the exercise of the reasoning powers. The woman, who has less in these particulars was given more of the spiritual and emotional nature and also an intuition by which she could understand the existence of things just as accurately and even more quickly than could the man by the exercise of his reasoning powers. One was just as the other in respect to the gifts bestowed and together they were the perfect pair—male and female created with diverse functions and duties to perform in the perfect workings of the laws of God.

Power and love were theirs and neither was made the superior of the other, nor was the one to be subject to the other and, had it not been for their fall, there never would have been the subjection of the female by the male. With their disobedience and subsequent fall, the animal qualities asserted themselves. The male felt his superiority by reason of the fact that he possessed a greater amount of these animal qualities, and the female became subordinated and has continued to be ever afterwards. As men degenerated, this domination intensified and for many thousands of years the inequality between male and female continued and man remained the master. This degradation continued until man found the lowest place of his degeneracy. When the turning point came, the qualities of the woman became more recognized, but very slowly.

The Jews recognized the equality of the woman in all matters which pertain to the home and the domestic life. However, men continued the distinction which had previously existed in respect to public affairs and the qualities of the mind. Women were not permitted to develop their mental faculties and were taught that all matters pertaining to the state or the religion of the race belonged to the male. As a result of this course of life the woman developed the spiritual qualities which were hers to a larger extent and her refinement and emotional nature and love principle exceeded those of the man to a great degree, and she became in her soul nearer the image of the Divine.

As the time approaches when man shall return to his former state of purity and harmony with the laws of God, the spiritual qualities will assert themselves and the animal qualities will become subordinated. Then the women will be recognized not only by the individual man but by the man-made laws as his equal in every particular, and the further fact will appear that she will be his superior in matters pertaining to the spiritual. Then the woman will stand before God and man as the latter's equal but, in the soul qualities, his superior; for in the beginning, in this particular, she was his superior.

Human Soul

Life on earth is an important part of the great eternity of living and should not be thought of as a mere stopping place where the spirit is enfolded in the flesh only for its pleasures and gratification. The earth life is a fleeting shadow of the spirit life but is the most important period of man's whole existence, and the way a life is lived on earth will determine its future existence.

The physical part of humans is the result of the meeting of those forces which are contained in the two sexes and, according to the laws of nature, are suited to produce the one body fit to be the home of the soul that is destined for it. The body which results from this meeting is intended only as a temporary vehicle for the growth of the soul and does not in any way limit or influence its continuous existence. The body, of itself, has neither consciousness nor sensation and in its beginning has only the borrowed life of its parents, and can exist only so long as the soul inhabits it. The physical body was never created to live forever and men were never created to live on the earth forever for a greater and larger world has been provided for their eternal habitation where things are real and only the spiritual exists. When the body's functions have ceased, it is disintegrated back into the elements from which it was formed.

The earth is a mere image of the realities of the spirit world and exists only as the nursery for the individualizing of the soul. The human soul is a creation of God and not an emanation or projection from God. It was created in the image and likeness of its Creator (Genesis 1:27), although not of the Creator's Essence or Substance, but of the matter which already existed as part of the spiritual universe. The creation of the human soul took place long before the appearance of mortals in the flesh. Prior to that appearance the soul had its existence in the spirit world as a substantial conscious entity without visible form or individuality, yet with a distinct personality so that each soul was different from all others and it had a consciousness of its existence and of its relationship to its Creator.

When the time comes for the soul to become an indweller in the mortal frame, it divides into two separate component parts, the male half incarnates into a male body and the female half incarnates into a female body and not necessarily at the same time. This separation is required for the individualization of each part of the one complete soul, yet the two parts never lose that inter-relationship or their binding qualities that existed before their separation.

God created male and female souls for the purpose of providing happiness for His children. Often soulmates do find each other, but due to differences in education, upbringing, customs and social mores, soulmates may be found but not necessarily acquired until the love possessed by the higher is achieved by the lower. Mere intellectual acquirement is not sufficient to attract and bring soulmates together; only love in perfect harmony can bring about this union. If it is not accomplished on earth, it can be in the spirit world; then the two parts of the one soul may progress together through the spheres of love and happiness.

I know that it is believed because of man's greatness that he has in him a portion of God's Divine Essence. This, however, is not the case for those qualities which appear to be of the Divine resemblance are merely those qualities which were created for the purpose of making man the highest and most perfect of all God's creations. Granted, there are certain qualities which man possesses such as love, wisdom and the reasoning faculties which may be said to resemble the God-like attributes, and so they do, but they are not a part of God's Essence or qualities, but they are merely made in their image and likeness.

With physical death comes the breaking of the silver cord and with that all connection between the soul and the physical body is severed for all eternity. The soul is protected by the spirit body which of itself is a creation just as the physical body is a creation. The spirit body exists only for the purpose of preserving man's individuality and to contain and shelter his soul both while on earth and after he becomes a spirit. When the soul is liberated from the body, its existence forevermore will be in its spirit body. The soul does not have of itself the power to determine its own location or destiny for the laws of attraction and compensation operate to make this determination.

There is no "angry" and "wrathful" God sitting in judgement, waiting to pronounce a sentence on the spirit who has left his earth life behind. The new spirit is met by spirit friends and relatives with love and kindness and consolation. This consolation is real for if it were not the lonely spirit would experience fear and bewilderment and the unspeakable sensation of being deserted. But, eventually the parting must come and every spirit must find its home according to its condition. Then comes a time when every spirit must stand alone in its weakness or strength and realize that no other spirit can bear its sorrows or take from it its burdens or enter into its sufferings. No interposition of spirit friends or the love of parents or husband or children can prevent this just destiny. Although for a time until the spirit has had an awakening to its condition of severance from the mortal life, these relatives and friends may retain it near the place of its entrance into the spirit world even though that place may be one of more beautiful surroundings and happiness than the one for which that spirit is destined. But this orientation does not last long for the law operates and as the spirit comes into full consciousness, it hears the call and must obey. There is no final destiny because the condition of the spirit is never fixed; as its condition changes, its destiny changes, and thus, there is an ever-continuing opportunity for the soul to progress.

The incarnation of the human soul into the flesh is just the first step in the soul's destined progress from an invisible formless existence to a perfected spirit. A soul in this process never retraces its steps; its movement is always forward; however, stagnation can occur for a time, but the soul always continues as an individualized spirit in pursuit of ultimate perfection and the great goal of union and oneness with its Creator.

Who and What is God

God is both Yahweh and Jehovah of the Jewish Scriptures and, at the same time, is the Heavenly Father who is referred to in the New Testament. This is despite the fact that Yahweh is a God of "wrath" and "vengeance", and the Heavenly Father is a God of Love, tenderness and mercy. Yet they are both the same unseen, true God, the creator of mankind who has always been "One" and changeless.

God revealed Himself first to Abraham in the Near East, but not for the first time in the entire world for the Orientals were really the first who had a perception of the true, unseen God. The development of the concept of Jehovah among the Hebrews came through an understanding of His laws of conduct toward men. This was brought to a higher level through Moses who led the Hebrew people out of slavery in Egypt. Their liberation was brought about as a result of their great sufferings and their inheritance of God as a religious concept. At this time the Hebrews were in a state in which they could be used as a whole people as witnesses of the existence of the invisible God.

The Exodus showed the power and love of God in bringing out of slavery an entire people, numbering many thousands, through the inspiration and courage which He gave to His instrument Moses. Many of the legends concerning Moses, it is true, are only stories. However, the fact remains that Moses did lead the people of Israel from Egypt after forcing the reluctant consent of Pharaoh and guided them hundreds of miles for many years to Mt. Sinai. There at Mt. Sinai in the name of the Most High, Moses gave the tablets of the Ten Commandments to the people. Moses could not have accomplished this great Exodus of the Hebrew Nation without the help of the living God of the Hebrews, Yahweh.

Many of the Hebrews believed in gods other than the one which Moses declared as is evidenced in their histories both sacred and secular. Whenever their God, that is, the God of Moses, did not treat them just as they thought He should, they would create and worship other gods, even the golden calf. To this day I admire Moses' closeness to God and his faith and courage in steadfastly obeying His commands. As a boy in Nazareth, I participated with my parents and brothers and sisters in the observance of the Passover which commemorates this important event.

The Old Testament writings reveal God as the Divinity that rules the universe and, in the narrower sense, the physical world of the earth and of man, and is the arbiter between man and his fellow beings. The prophets of Israel contributed to the elevation of the spiritual concepts of the nation and gave the people and their leaders a deeper insight into the real nature of the Lord. This is to be found in the prophet Nathan who appeared fearlessly before David, the king, to accuse him of murder and adultery in his relations with Bathsheba. It was Elijah who braved the haughty Jezebel and showed the power provided especially for him by Angel spirits to show the power of the unseen, eternal God in contest with the priests of Baal. And it was Amos who came to the priests at Gilead to warn the Israelites to repent of their sins, mainly the sins of the rich and powerful who abused the poor and brought them to misery and slavery.

From these prophets the people were able to understand that God wanted righteousness and mercy in the dealings with other human beings, not only amongst their own people but for all people including the stranger within their gates for they, too, had been strangers in other's lands. The people had been taught to trust in the one unseen and eternal God and to know Him through His attributes and laws which were the guides the Jews were to follow in their relations with others and in conducting all their affairs. They were given to understand that God was Ruler, not only of the Jews but of all human beings, and that He was to be obeyed.

God is the Almighty, who is omnipotent, omniscient and omnificent and as such, has no limitations as a sexual concept, namely father-soul or mother-soul, nor can any human expression in truth be applied to God. When I refer to God as my "Father", I do this to indicate the fact that I am at-one with Him in nature through my possession of His Divine Love, and I make no reference to any qualities that represent human maleness or masculinity for these should not be applied to God.

There is nothing in all of nature which men are acquainted with or have knowledge of which can be used to make a comparison to God. For humans to conceive that God has a form in any manner resembling that of man is erroneous, and those who in their beliefs and teachings deny the anthropomorphic God are correct. The true form of God has never been conceived of by men in all the ages including those who believe in the Bible of the Hebrews as well as in that of the Christians.

God is of a form which gives Him an entity and substance and seat of habitation in contradistinction to that God who, in the teachings of some men, is said to be everywhere and in everything—in the rocks and trees, in thunder and lightning, in man and beasts, in all created things and in that in which man is said to live and move and have his being. No, this concept of God is not in accord with the truth, and it is vital to the knowledge and redemption of man that such a conception of God not be entertained or believed in. To believe that God is without form is to believe that God is a mere force or principle or nebulous power or, as some say, the resultant of laws, which laws have been established by God for the controlling of His universe of creation. These laws are expressed to men by these very powers and principles to the extent that man can comprehend. God is behind force, principle and law which are the expressions of His Being and without Him they could not exist. They are changeable, dependent and subject to the will of God.

I am enabled by my soul perceptions to see God and

His form, but here I use the words "see" and "form" to be the only words that I can use to give mortals a comparative conception of what I am endeavoring to describe. Mortals can scarcely conceive the form of the spirit body of man which is composed or formed of the material of the universe though it is usually not accepted to be of such material. It is hardly possible for me to convey to mortals a faint idea of the Soul form of God which is composed of that which is purely spiritual—that is, not of physical material, even if it were sublimated to the highest degree.

God is a Soul. Not the soul that is in the created human, but the soul that is Deity, self-existent and whose entity is the one great fact in the universe of being. It is a mistake for men to believe that because God has created this or that object or thing, that it is necessarily a part of Himself. God's creations are no more a part of Himself than are the creations of men a part of themselves and thus you will see that in all of God's creation there is nothing of the Divine except the souls of His children who have sought for and have been privileged to partake of His Divine Love.

God has His locality from where He works out His purposes and makes Himself and the evidence of His existence known to man by the energies that control the universe in which man exists. God is of a form that can only be seen by the soul perceptions of a man who has arrived at a high degree of spiritual development and who has taken on God's Divine Nature. To others, God is unseen and unknown except as His laws and the effect of their operation disclose His Being. It must be realized that just because men cannot understand or perceive the truth of God 's great Soul, that does not mean it is not a truth. A truth, though not conceived or perceived by men, spirits or Angels, is still a truth and its existence does not depend upon its being known to them.

In addition God has a personality and this is expressed and made known to men by certain attributes which to the consciousness of man are existent in the universe. God is not with men in this personality yet He is with them in His attributes of wisdom, knowledge, power, goodness, mercy and will. Life emanates from God, but life is not God, it is only one of His attributes that He has conferred upon the objects of His creation. In this way man may live and grow and fulfill the purpose of his design.

Now to some philosophers and scientists and scholars these attributes "are" their impersonal God Himself and to them the only God. They mistakenly make the created, the Creator, not realizing that behind the expression must be the cause and greater than the expression must be that from which it emanates or, as some believe, evolved. I, who know, desire to say that these manifested attributes or forces and powers and principles and laws and expressions are not and do not altogether constitute that from which they flow or in which they have their source. God is Himself alone. His attributes or expressions manifested to mortals and spirits are the results or effects of the workings of his spirit, and this spirit is the active energy of His Soul. Hence, the form of God is not distributed throughout the whole universe where His attributes are because God's spirit is manifested everywhere.

As was said by Moses of old and as was said by me when on earth, God is in His Heaven, and it may be surprising and startling for mortals to hear, God has His habitation and, God the Substance, the self-existing Soul form, has His locality, and men do not live and move and have their existence in God but in His emanations and expressions and spirit they do.

Prayer and Faith

God is Love and they that worship Him in the spirit of love will not be forsaken. I am my Father's Son and am not to be worshiped as God. To make me the object of worship and to put God in the background is all wrong.

So I say you must love the Lord thy God with all your heart and soul and mind and your neighbor as yourself (Mark 12:30-31) and send your prayers to God in the name of truth. If any name must be used in supplication then use "only" the name of the Father for His name is high over all and the only name under heaven or earth that can bring salvation to man.

What I have said applies to many other declarations contained in the Bible such as, "he that believeth on the Lord Jesus Christ shall be saved" (Acts 15:11), and "there is no other name under heaven whereby men can be saved" (Acts 4:12). These are the enunciations of a false doctrine which is misleading to a great majority of people who accept these declarations as literally true. Of course, if they are interpreted to mean he who believes in the truths that I teach, then the objection is not so great. Even then, the declarations do not go far enough for people may believe in these truths and that belief may be a mere mental one, acquiesced by the mind's faculties without any exercise of the soul's senses. If, to this mental belief be added the soul's faith, then this doctrine will be truly stated and man will understand what is necessary for redemption.

Belief and faith are not the same. Belief is of the mind, faith is of the soul. Belief can and does change as phenomena and apparent facts change. Faith, when truly possessed, never changes for faith possessed by a soul causes all the longings and aspirations of that soul to become things of real existence, as the house that is built upon solid rock can never be shaken or destroyed (Matthew 7:24). Believe in God and trust in me for you will not be disappointed and pray for Divine Love to enter your soul so that you will know that you are an accepted child of God.

Of all the important things on earth for those who are seeking salvation, happiness and development of the soul, prayer is the most important. Whenever the opportunity presents itself, you should pray. By this I mean you need not wait for a special time when you are not engaged in daily affairs, but pray when you can seize moments when your mind is free even if only for a second. A long prayer or even one formulated into words is not necessary with the longing words need not be used. The longing is quicker than the thought and sending your longings heavenward will bring results.

God is always open and ready to respond to such longings, even just one second of true soul-felt prayer with the soul's longings active is more effective than hours of prayer when such longings are not present. Prayers of the lip or of habit rise no higher than the escaping breath and do not cause the Divine Love to flow into the human soul. Remember this and realize how futile are all prayers when the soul's longings and desires are not present. Only soul can call to Soul, and the Holy Spirit will respond only when such a soul calls. No mediator is needed, nor prayers or ceremonies of priests or preachers for God comes to His children Himself and hears their prayers and responds by sending His Comforter.

Prayers call from God a response that brings Divine Love, and with It comes faith and the awareness that a new Love is growing in one's soul. Many people understand such faith to be mere belief, but it is greater than belief and exists in its true sense only in the soul. Belief may arise from a conviction of the mind, but faith never can. When you pray to God to increase your faith, it is a prayer for the increase of Divine Love. Faith is based on the possession of this Love and gives the aspirations and longings of the soul real living existence. Faith is not the belief produced from the mere operation of the mind, but comes from the opening of the perceptions of the soul.

God answers prayers to help those who seek Him to overcome their unfavorable material conditions through His ministering Angels and spirits. These spirits are always watching and working and, when the opportunity arises, they use their influence in the best possible way to bring about the ends desired. If the prayers of men can be responded to, they are; however, should a man come to God seeking power and assistance in say, the murder of a fellow human, no matter how great an enemy that man might be, God will not give power or assistance or approve of such a desire. Nor does God by a mere act of the moment or of a physical character place into the hands of men riches or prosperity. These things must be wrought and brought about by man himself. However, the workings of God's spirits aid men in a wonderful way to cause him to act in compliance with their influence. This influence is always used for the purpose to bring about a response to prayers which in their nature are proper and worthy to be answered.

The material or earth plane conditions are not subject to spiritual laws but to material laws; yet, in a time of need, the person with faith who prays to God for help will be kept in contact with the spirit forces that will give strength and courage in this time of adversity. Spirits can also help mortals because they can know what will happen in the near future and can tell mortals what may be expected or rather what will occur. Prayers can remove worry from the aspirant's consciousness. This is accomplished by God operating in such a way to remove the effect of the cause of worry on the feelings and mental conditions of the individual.

God gave humans free will to act and, by that very gift, took away from Himself the absolute power to force any human to do as He wishes. God cannot nor does not force humans to act contrary to their desires even though they may be for unmitigated evil. God never makes a mistake in the perfection of His creatures even though in the case of man it may appear that He did when he gave man the great power of free will which in its wrongful exercise has caused sin and evil to appear in the world of man's consciousness.

There are universal laws God created which He cannot or will not nullify even to protect life. What He can do is to bring into operation higher laws which, if obeyed, may neutralize those in effect in answer to sincere prayer. Thus, I say pray not only for material things which He bestows through His Angels and spirits, but also for spiritual things which God bestows through His Holy Spirit.

Forgiveness

I would like to enlighten you on a subject which is so little understood since men first commenced to distort my teachings on the forgiveness and pardon of the Father.

Forgiveness is that operation of the Heavenly Father which relieves men of the penalties for the sins they have committed and permits them to turn from evil thoughts and deeds to seek God's Love and find the happiness that is waiting for them. The law of compensation, "that what a man sows that shall he also reap" (Galatians 6:7), is not set aside but, in the particular case in which a man becomes penitent and in all earnestness prays to God, the operation of another and greater law is called into activity. The old law of compensation is nullified as though it were swallowed up by the power of the higher law of Love (Romans 13:10).

God sees every act of man and, as I said when I was on earth, not even a sparrow falls without my Father's knowing it, and the hairs of your head are all numbered (Matthew 10:29-30). Just because men cannot see God, it does not mean that God does not see them for He does and their every thought is known to Him and taken into account. Surprising as it may seem, that account is kept in the memories and consciences of men themselves, and when the time comes for them to render an account of their acts and thoughts, no other place or receptacle is sought for or examined to find this account than these very memories. The memory is man's storehouse of good and evil, and the memory does not die with the death of the physical body. On the contrary it becomes more active and alive and nothing is left behind or forgotten when man casts off the encumbrance and the benumbing and deceiving influences of the mortal flesh.

The suffering for sins committed is not the result of God's special condemnation, but in each particular case is the result of the workings and scourging of the conscience and recollections. As long as the conscience works, the suffering will continue and, the greater the sins committed, the greater will be the suffering. This implies that a soul filled to a greater or lesser extent with these memories for the time these memories will constitute his very existence. He lives with these memories and the suffering and torment which result from them can not leave him until the memories of these sins, or the result of them, cease to be a part of him and his constant companion—this is the inexorable law of compensation.

In the spirit world when a man has committed sins on earth, the law of compensation demands that he must pay the penalty to the last farthing. There is no forgiveness until the individual makes the effort by struggling and succeeding to get rid of these recollections and such riddance can be obtained only by the opening of the soul and the feeling of remorse and regret for the evils he had done. God will respond for it is true that God helps those who help themselves and when God forgives, sin disappears and then only Love exists, and this Love in its fullness is the fulfillment of the law. When this Love enters the soul of man, It increases as the leaven in dough and continues in its work until the whole soul is impregnated with It, and then everything of sin or error is wholly eradicated.

God knows no preference and had no chosen people in the sense that He designed to save any particular nation in preference to all others. All are His children, however, He does not forgive them by a sudden blotting out of their sins, so you should understand that neither can the popes, priests or preachers by the mere pronouncing of forgiveness. This would constitute a deception and an injury to the penitent who prays and asks for forgiveness. These men will have to answer for this when they go to the spirit world and realize the truth of forgiveness and the great deception they have practiced upon those who were their followers and believers in their false doctrines.

Teaching the understanding of God's forgiveness was one of the objects of my mission. Before I came and taught this great truth, the forgiveness of sin was not understood even by the Hebrew teachers but their doctrine was an eye for an eye and a tooth for a tooth. The Divine Love, as I have described, was not known or sought for; but only the care and protection and material benefits that God might give to the Hebrew people.

The Two Loves

I want you to know that there are two loves in the universe and not merely one. The human or natural love is the love of the physical universe and the Divine Love is the Love of the spiritual universe.

The love of man or natural love is not one that is sufficient to give the highest degree of happiness which he may obtain in either the mortal life or in the spirit life. This love is of a nature that changes with the change in the ideas and desires of men and has no stability that will serve to keep him constant in his affections. The natural love is one that may last for a long time, and sometimes it seems that it can never die or grow less; yet, in its very nature, it has not that constancy which insures its lasting longer than a moment of time. Mother's love is the strongest of all loves given to mortals, and apparently it can never end or grow old, yet a time may come when that love will die or cease to retain all its vitality and beauty.

The natural love need not be prayed for or acquired because every human has it endowed in his soul at the time of its creation. However, this love is not in its original pristine condition as it first appeared on earth in the souls of the First Parents, it has become tainted since their fall and needs to be purified and expressed through kind thoughts and deeds, patience, forgiveness, mercy, generosity and caring. Natural love is the driving force behind all human love—motherly love, brotherly love and its highest expression, soulmate love. These loves are provisions of God which are necessary to enable man to work out his progress through the mortal life and in a way that will produce the greatest harmony and happiness among mortals as they contend with the difficulties, cares and disappointments of their earthly existences.

The Divine Love is very different in substance and quality than the human love and is not the development of the human love but It is the Essence of what Love is, whereas the human or natural love is made merely in the image and likeness of the Divine Love. The Divine Love was never conferred upon man as a perfected and completed gift at the time of his creation, but it is a gift which is waiting to be obtained through effort and aspiration. It is not a part of man's nature but can be obtained and possessed since the time of my coming by all who seek for It. God has always been the same with the exception of giving His Love with my appearance on earth when the Father revealed Himself truly in revealing His greatest attribute—Divine Love which is also His Nature.

Divine Love comes from without and is not developed from within. It is the result of individual acquirement and not the object of universal possession. It may be possessed by all or it may be possessed by only a few; each man must determine that for himself. It is not a matter of right, nor is It ever forced upon one. It is greater than faith or hope because It is the real Substance of the Soul of God.

There is no royal road to obtain Divine Love, all must pursue It in the same way as I taught when I was on earth. As the soul opens to God through sincere prayer and longing, Divine Love flows from God's Soul to the human soul and is carried by the Holy Spirit. Once implanted It finds lodgment therein for all eternity. It may lay dormant for a time but can be awakened when the soul desires.

When humans possess Divine Love, they possess everything that will make them not only perfect humans but Divine Angels as well. Then they will understand the moral precepts of brotherly love and also the "Oneness" of God. They will not have to seek further for those qualities that bring peace and goodwill but will know that every other soul is their brother. Envy, hatred, strife, jealousy and all other evil qualities will disappear and only peace, joy and happiness will remain. Then they will be able to do unto each other as they would have the other do unto them (Luke 6:31) without effort or sacrifice on their part for love worketh its own fulfillment and all its beneficence.

In summation, Divine Love is the greatest thing in all of the universe and not only the greatest, but the sum of all things for from It flows every other thing that brings peace, love and happiness. I am a progressive spirit and as I grew in love and knowledge and wisdom while on earth, I am still growing in these qualities in the spirit world. When the Love and mercy and goodness of the Heavenly Father comes to me, it comes with all the assurance that never in all eternity will I cease to progress towards the very Fountainhead of God's Divine Love, the only God, the All-in-All.

Jesus

Jesus of the Bible

Psychic Influences in the Bible

Compiled by Austin D. Wallace 1951

Apports

Numbers 11:31 17:8
Psalms 78:24
Ezekiel 2:9

Casting Out Spirits

I Samuel 16:23
Matthew 8:16
Mark 5:8
Acts 5:16 8:7 16:18 19:12

Clairaudience

Ezekiel 13:13

Clairvoyance

Genesis 15:1
Exodus 24:10
II Kings 6:12
Jeremiah 1:11,13
Ezekiel 8:3
Daniel 2:19 3:25
John 21:6
Acts 9:10,12 16:9

Dreams

Genesis 28:12 31:11, 24
37:5,9
Samuel 28:15
Job 33:15
Matthew 1:20 2:13 27:19

Fire Manifestations

Genesis 19:24
Exodus 3:2 14:24
Judges 15:14
Daniel 3:22
Acts 2:3 7:30

Gift of Healing

Matthew 10:8

Luke 9:2 10:9
I Corinthians 12:9 12:28

Healings

I Kings 17:22
II Kings 4:35 5:14
Matthew 8:13 12:13
Luke 5:17 9:11 17:14
John 5:8-9
Acts 3:7-8 9:18 14:10
28:8-9

Holy Spirit

Joel 2:28
Acts 2:4,17 4:31 9:17

Independent Spirit Voice

Genesis 21:17 22:11,15
Exodus 19:3 20:1
Judges 2:1 13:3
I Samuel 3:4 9:15
I Kings 19:5
Job 4:12
Ezekiel 1:24, 25, 28 13:13
Matthew 17.5
John 12: 28-30
Acts 7:31 9:7 11:7-9

Independent Writing

Exodus 24:12 31:18 34:1
Deuteronomy 9:10
II Chronicles 21:12
Daniel 5:5

Inspirational Speaking

Mark 13:12

Levitation

I Kings 18:12

Ministering of Angels

Genesis 21:7 32:1,24
Joshua 5:13-14
I Kings 19:5-7
Luke 1:26 2:9,13 4:10
Acts 5:19 8:26 12:7

Names of Controls

Genesis 32:29
Judges 13:17
Job 26:4
Mark 5:9

Physical Phenomena

Genesis 30:30
Exodus 4:3
Judges 6:40
I Kings 19:5-7,11,12
II Kings 3:15
Matthew 8:26
Acts 12:7

Prophesy

Exodus 4:17
I Samuel 10:6
Ezekiel 14:13
Luke 1:67-68

Seances

John 20:19
Acts 2:1-4

Spirit Guidance

Exodus 4:15-16
Acts 11:12
Galatians 2:2

Spirit Light

Genesis 15:17

Exodus 34:29
Ezekiel 1:28
Acts 9:3

Spirit Manifestation

Genesis 3:8 18:1 19:1
I Samuel 28:13-14
II Kings 3:15
Ezekiel 2:2
Luke 1:11
John 21:4,14

Spirit Materialization

I Kings 19:6
Luke 25:15-16
Acts 26:16

Spirit Power

Daniel 6:22
Matthew 28:2
Acts 5:19

Spiritual Gifts

Daniel 2:26
John 14:26
Act.s 2:17
Luke 10:19-20
I Corinthians 12:1,4

Tongues

I Corinthians 14:18

Trance

Genesis 15:12
Numbers 24:4
Daniel 8:18 10:9
Acts 10:10 22:17

Trumpet Mediumship

Revelations 1:10 4:1

THE LOST TEACHINGS FROM JESUS

BOOK LIST

I hope you found *The Genuine Jesus* of interest. If so, I am certain you will find the books of its origin listed below of equal or even greater interest. I invite you to examine the book list and consider reading from this great storehouse of knowledge that has been concealed since the beginning of the century. All books contain messages from Jesus and were received by automatic writing.

1. **The Genuine Jesus** 1998 Paperback 96 pgs. 50 messages
. . . . $7.95 / £5.95
Compiled from the writings of James E. Padgett and his successor Dr. Daniel G. Samuels. The story of Jesus' life from his birth and formative years, to his ministry, death and resurrection. Told in the first person by Jesus this autobiography is a revelation of the New Testament.

True Gospel Revealed Anew by James Padgett
(Published by The Foundation Church of the New Birth)

2. **Volume 1** 1940 Paperback 383 pgs. 102 messages
. . . . $14.95 / £9.50
This first volume offers a comprehensive introduction by its British publisher, Dr. Leslie R. Stone. It contains the most powerful of all the messages from Jesus: they cover the nature of the human soul, atonement, forgiveness, heaven and hell, the Holy Spirit, who and what is God and much more.

3. **Volume 2** 1954 Paperback 391 pgs. 285 messages
. . . . $14.95 / £9.50
The messages in this volume reveal spiritual insight not found elsewhere. In them the disciples describe events in Palestine with their Master. There are also fascinating messages from Lazarus, Nicodemus, Josephus, Emanuel Swedenborg, Martin Luther, Abraham Lincoln, Francis Bacon, Mary Baker Eddy and many others.

4. **Volume 3** 1969 Paperback 404 pgs. 408 messages
. . . . $14.95 / £9.50
This volume contains messages from the famous and not so famous from many lands and many times. They tell of their lives on the earth, all well as their lives, homes, work and pleasures in the spirit world. It also contains messages from White Eagle, William Gladstone, Rev. Stainton Moses, Lafayette, Clara Barton and Thomas Payne among others.

5. **New Testament Revelations** 1966 Dr. Daniel G. Samuels
Oversize 125 pgs. 53 messages . . . . $9.95 / £6.50
Received by James Padgett's successor. This provocative
collection of messages reinterprets many important subjects of the
New Testament. They also elaborate on the Oahspe Bible, the
Shroud of Turin, reincarnation and spiritual healing.

6. **Old Testament Sermons** 1957 Dr. Daniel G. Samuels
Vol 1 & 2 Oversize 100 pgs. 76 messages . . . .$9.95 / £6.50
This book contains a wealth of historical information and religious
knowledge for those students of the Old Testament.

ORDERING INFORMATION

IN THE UK

To order *The Genuine Jesus* within the U.K. please post a sterling
cheque for £5.95 plus .85p shipping per copy payable to: Two Worlds
Publishing, 7 The Leather Market, Weston Street, London SE1 3ER.
You may also order by credit card (with the exception of Switch and
American Express), by faxing to 0171- 378 0808 or e-mail
tortzen@globalnet.co.uk Please include your name, address, type of
card, expiry date and title of book. For orders of *The Genuine Jesus*
outside the UK and EC countries from Two Worlds Publishing, please
add an extra £1.00 for postage.

FROM THE U.S

Books other than *The Genuine Jesus* are available only from the U.S.
Please add the following postage to the price of the book or books you
desire.

The Genuine Jesus: Postage within the U.S. surface $1.25 air $2.00 ea.
Postage to the U.K. surface £1.75 air £2.50 ea.

The Volumes: Within the U.S. surface $1.60 air $3.20 ea.
To the U.K. surface £1.75 air £4.50 ea.

The New Testament Revelations & Old Testament Sermons:
Within the U.S. surface $1.60 air $3.20 ea.
To the U.K. surface £1.75 air £4.50 ea.

Please note: With air service Volumes, Revelations and Sermons two
books can go for the cost of one.

PAYMENT INFORMATION

Residents of the US, UK, Canada, Australia and New Zealand please pay with your country check, money order or credit card. All other countries please use the pound cost for books and postage and convert your currency to pounds or dollars at the current exchange rate. Orders within the state of California please add 8.25% sales tax. Mail the form below to the most convenient address in the front of the book, or to order by credit card (Visa and Master Card only) phone or fax (888) 937-0411 or e-mail alanross@aol.com Thank you very much.

ORDER FORM

Item #	Book Title	Quantity	Price

Sub Total ....

Postage ....

Grand Total ....

Name ....

Address ....

....

....

Country ....

Phone .... e-mail ....

QUESTIONNAIRE

I hope you have enjoyed *The Genuine Jesus*. Your opinion of it is important to me. I would be grateful if you would please fill in the form below and mail it to the most convenient address in the front of the book. Thank you.

1. I believe this story to be: completely true ....
   mostly true .... slightly true .... not true at all ....

2. I believe the spirit author to be Jesus of the Bible:
   yes .... no .... perhaps .... not sure........

3. It was thought provoking and held my interest:
   1 2 3 4 5 6 7 8 9 10

4. I would be willing to tell others about *The Genuine Jesus*.
   yes .... no ....

5. I would be interested to start or attend a study group or
   to help arrange for Alan to speak at my church.
   yes .... no ....

Your Additional Comments:

....
....
....
....
....
....
....

Name: ....

Address: ....

....

....

Country: ....

Phone.. e-mail ....